Angel Star Cat

Angel Star Cat

A Mystical Journey Through The Storms Of Life With An Enchanted Cat And His Mom.

Karla Wessel

Aventine Press

First Edition
Published 2005

Editor: Hazel Houle
Cover Art and Final Editor: Rebecca LeTourneau
Interior photos and illustrations: Karla Wessel and Eric Houle

Published by Aventine Press
1023 4th Ave #204
San Diego CA, 92101
www.aventinepress.com

ISBN: 1-59330-275-4

Library of Congress Control Number: 2005926131
Library of Congress cataloging-in-Publication Data
Wessel, Karla Angel Star Cat, by Karla Wessel and Pierre
Bibliography: 1. Spiritual Guidance, 2. Animals and Pets,
3. Rites and Ceremonies I. Title II. Series

Printed in the United States of America

Pierre's Dedication

To all of the animals, birds, fish and creatures of this world;
this is our book! Each of us is needed here on earth.
We help by continually bringing love,
to this universe.
Pierre, the French Birman Cat

Karla's Dedication

To my angel cat, Pierre, and to all the many kinds of angels
in the universe who have helped me realize the importance of
their divine assistance. I dedicate this book to you. Pierre was
a special angel cat sent to teach me celestial lessons. He is
the one who got this whole project going.
Karla Wessel, Pet Mom

Pierre's Acknowledgments

Thank you, Karla, for seeing the light and understanding that my book must be written now. Thank you for finally realizing that we are writing this book together and that your stories connect with my own. Many thanks also to my pet family: Joe, Karla, Caroline, Forrest, Hazel and Eric, for loving and caring for me. I love you all. Meow, Meow, Meow!
  Pierre

Karla's Acknowledgments

I wish to thank Figaro, Tiger, Lassie, Elbirdo, Tip, Billy, Rowdy, Lemon, Dozer, Casper, Lizzie, Kleenex, Cotton, Streakers, Prince, Joker, Monica and Pierre for being in my life throughout the years and for bringing me such joy.

Angel Star Cat is written in memory of my parents who taught me to persevere when meeting many challenges in life, maintaining always a sense of humor, kindness, honesty and determination. I know they would be proud of me for writing this book, especially since Dad and Mom taught me to love animals and nature.

I also wish to thank my brother and sister who have always been there for me, even when baffled by my eccentric ways. They have been a marvelous support.

To my children Caroline, Forrest, Hazel and Eric, I thank you for being four beaming angels in my life, bringing me endless inspiration and delight. Thanks to Caroline for editing at the beginning of this project, to Forrest for his expertise with computers, to Hazel for editing of my entire book at the end of this project and to Eric for his wonderful art work.

To my friends the Seven Sisters, whom I have known all of my life – my sister Nan, Sandy Rosove, Sue Paine, Jeannie Soebbing, Marge Stresemann, Christie Macintosh, who is no longer with us, and Marie Lunzer, Jerry Kester, Marge Lauber, Debbie Oaks, Jackie Wessel, June Paschke, Shirley Larsen, Cheryl Smith, Mary Chapman, Bright Star, Jeanne Crescenzo, Julie Whaley, Rock Patty, Karen Miller, Karen Neihart, and in loving memory of Betty Klein and Mary Rowan; I thank all of you for your support and positive thoughts.

To Becky LeTourneau, who came in near the end of this project, I also thank you for your understanding and constant help to finish this book. Your editing and good ideas have helped to carry this project to the end.

Lastly, and most of all, I thank Joe my soul mate, who ultimately acknowledged the importance of having our indoor cat Pierre. Joe is my greatest love, friend and partner. He has always been supportive and has encouraged me in my many endeavors, always having faith in me. I encountered unbelievable adversity with getting this first book done, but still managed to prevail with faith, a sense of humor and great determination. Joe's sense of humor and patience with his unusual wife have carried him through many challenges in life with me!

Karla

Contents

Preface — by Pierre

I am a nineteen year old French Birman cat. In this lifetime I am a gray and white longhair cat with baby blue eyes – and quite charming and debonair, if I do say so myself! The week I became very sick, my pet mom called a veterinarian, who thankfully made house calls. I was nervous about seeing a stranger yet instinctively knew she was going to try to help me so I did not hide under a bed like I usually do when people come over. I felt she loved animals so I let her examine me.

I wondered what was wrong with me. I felt very tired and had to use my pussycat powder room a lot. I know I am getting older but it is comforting to realize my symptoms are normal for an elderly cat. Now I am on a diet of healthier cat food and am taking medicine for my kidneys along with some pills for my arthritis. Even though my pet mom crushes the pills, I can still taste them in tuna or in any of my other favorite treats. Whom does she think she is fooling? She tries to hide them but we have not found a satisfactory way for me to take those pills. We are still negotiating a good solution to this problem.

Still, one positive thing that has come out of this health crisis is that the spiritual connection between my pet mom and myself has become deeper than ever. Her gift to me is writing this book. I dictated it to her, tuning into her spirit as she wrote, bringing my thoughts into her heart and soul. Most of the time I sat on her lap, which was not easy with the computer right in front of her! I flashed thoughts and images from my world to hers so she could capture them in the words she wrote, and this book is the result of our heart to heart communication.

Anyone can talk with his or her pet. When you open your heart with loving thoughts toward your animals they respond and send messages back to you. This is communication at its best and I experienced it from the start with my pet mom. My gift to her is my unconditional love and appreciation for her being my pet mom and friend.

I was in her life years ago as Cotton, an outdoor cat, but could not get her to understand then how important it is for animals to communicate with humans. Several years later, as Pierre, I was finally in the house and could influence her more. As Pierre, I have been able to teach her about the messages from animals and nature.

My pet mom has always been intuitive and has done readings for many years. She had a vision a few years ago while atop a mountain, meditating and praying in Sedona, Arizona. She told me about this vision when she came back from her trip as I sat purring on her lap.

Pierre at work in Karla's office

Preface — by Karla

In April of 2002 Pierre became very ill, which made me realize I needed to talk more to him about how I felt about things while I still had the chance. I also wanted to thank him for being with me for so long and for being such a wonderful pet over the years. I have whispered many secrets to him during our times together. I had been working on another book but when Pierre became ill I realized we must write this book first, and that we should tell this story together!

I have been intuitive all my life, and with a special affinity for nature and animals. I met my Indian/angel spirit guide, Keeno, when I was about three years old. Over the course of my lifetime I have also met many other spirits and guides. Most recently I discovered an angel guide, Joyelle, and because of all these inspirational influences I am now creating paintings of these colorful spirits and angel cats.

My guides offer daily confirmation of the presence of angels. I have weathered many storms in life with the guidance of my loving spiritual companions. I believe one can either become stronger or can become a victim when facing challenges in life. I choose to be a survivor and learn the celestial lessons of life – of which there are many for each of us. I believe art is healing, and my work as an intuitive artist is my way of sharing the messages I receive from Spirit (often through animals).

I have traveled a lot but one of my most important trips was to Sedona, Arizona where I had an astounding vision while on a mountaintop. Sedona is a place of vortexes, which are high energy, psychic power spots. When I visit this place I feel much more in tune with the mysteries of other dimensions.

At the time I was working with Tarot cards, Runes and crystals. I set them before me as I sat cross legged on a huge red rock. As I was meditating and praying, Keeno appeared and told me to create my own cards for intuitive readings. A surge of powerful sizzling energy came through my whole body from head to toe. It hit me like a lightning bolt! I still get goose bumps when I remember this jubilant, joyful feeling racing through me.

I have always been a dreamer and many of my dreams are revelations or premonitions - a most powerful tool in my life. I returned to Minnesota and started having strong, intuitive dreams that seemed quite real. I dreamed 107 nights in a row, of animals, birds, flowers, fish and trees. Each of these images in the dreams talked to me, telling me its meaning. I awakened every morning with a new image and promptly drew it on my sketchpad to recapture it, writing down the explanation for the card, which I had received in my dream. I made this deck and started using it for the intuitive readings I was doing at the time.

It was a beautiful, calm, sunny day in late autumn when I finished retracing these cards for the final time. As I finished the last stroke, I asked the angels to give me a sign that I was on the right track with these cards. Immediately, all the lights in the house went out! I called the neighbors to see if their lights had gone out also but they were not having any such problem.

When the lights went back on, I realized the significance of this strange occurrence and thanked God for showing me the validation I was looking for. So often in my life Spirit has validated what I needed to know was true. Sometimes I have a tingling over my whole body. Other times I get goose bumps or chills, but whatever way it comes, confirmation from Spirit is always a marvelous gift.

I ordered purple mesh bags for the animal cards I had created. They arrived by UPS and just as I opened the box, I was drawn to look out our window that faces the lake. I knew intuitively there was going to be something wrong with the order and there was – the bags I received for my cards were white instead of the purple I had requested.

As I looked out of our bay window, I discovered about 100 seagulls on the lake where the ice was just starting to freeze over. I was ecstatic over my discovery of the birds as I felt they were a message from Spirit. They were like 100 angels arriving to inform me that these white bags were indeed the best color for my cards. I had printed my cards one week before and now had these white bags in which to put them. I felt that Spirit was communicating through the sea gulls. Sometimes unexpected changes are actually for the best. Always look for the good in life – this is a philosophy I share with Pierre.

Karla in Sedona, AZ

1

Meet the Family

Pierre's Philosophy

I have one paw that appears to have a gray stocking, which is not quite proper for a show cat according to some. When I was born with the markings I have, some thought me imperfect but one of the things that makes humans and animals so special is that we are all different and unique. As for me, I may have one gray stocking but I also have spectacular French charm and am rather dashing!

I chose my human family (which from my perspective is of course, really my pet family) because I knew they would be fun, interesting, loving and adventurous to live with. I was sure our time together would be a bold venture for all of us. My pet mom, Karla, is bright and kind and she really likes to play. She has been psychic all of her life but she needed a bit of a boost to muster up enough courage to start telling people what she saw and experienced. I am pleased to say that I was one of those boosts.

My pet parents, Karla and Joe, have been happily married for many years and raised four children together: Caroline, Forrest, Hazel, and Eric. Over the years, our family also had many pets that added their own unique personalities to our mix - dogs, cats, frogs, lizards, turtles, and even a tarantula - a most special lady. These animals enhanced my life and the lives of this family over the years.

A Rough Beginning

Years before I reincarnated into my current cat body and took the name Pierre, I was a cat named Cotton. In that lifetime I was a Himalayan cat with the same markings that I have now: gray paws and face, white body, and of course my sexy, beautiful, baby blue eyes. My original pet dad decided to get rid of my sister and me so he drove us into town and placed us inside a van that was parked in a parking lot. My sister and I did not know it yet but this van belonged to Joe, my future pet dad, who was busy at work and had no idea that two small kittens were now waiting outside in his vehicle. Later that night when he drove home, my sister and I were too scared to let out even the tiniest meow so Joe went on into the house completely unaware that two little kittens were now going to be sleeping in his van all night long.

The next morning, Joe drove the children to school like he did every morning on his way to work. By this time my poor little sister and I were scared, lonely, and exceedingly hungry so I gathered up my courage and decided to announce our presence. From beneath the back seat I opened my tiny mouth and let out a brave meow. Thankfully, it was enough to get the attention of this family which is how they finally discovered us.

Fortunately, Joe was able to give my sister to a student in the parking lot that day, someone responsible, who was also a friend of the family.

"Don't take me," I kept thinking as the children hovered around. I did not want to go with anyone else – I wanted to stay with this family! I felt very strongly that I was supposed to stay with this particular family for some reason. It must have been written in the stars because it turned out that Joe was thinking the same thing. Somehow, he knew instinctively that he should keep me and not my sister. It was his feeling that my sister would be happy with another family and I was the one who should be taken back to his home where he could introduce me to his wife Karla. And this is exactly what he did.

My new family named me Cotton and made a home for me outside in a small shed with a cat door. In this shed was a wooden house that was insulated and had carpeting and straw in it.

As Karla delighted in showering me with love, she kept wondering if I could be part Himalayan. Her heart told her I should be an indoor cat. She was right about that but did not trust herself enough at that time to fight for me and to make an issue of this with her husband.

Life Lessons

I lived for only five years in that lifetime. So many things can happen to an outdoor cat, especially if it is a fragile breed. My pet mom began to realize if she had another cat it should be allowed indoors. I was proud of the role I played as Cotton because in that lifetime I taught my pet mom to trust her intuition.

Caroline and Cotton

I wanted to teach her so many more things but knew I would have to come back again. This is why people and animals reincarnate - to develop a lesson, or karma, further along. What people do in this life can affect what their destiny will be in the next life, sort of like a giant boomerang. Animals and people who have been connected in one life will sometimes meet again in another life. This is the way it has been with Karla and me – first I knew her as Cotton, and then later, when she met me again, I was a cat named Pierre.

Cotton in the Baby Buggy

Caroline and Pierre

Forrest and Pierre

Hazel and Pierre

Eric and Pierre

Karla's Celestial Thoughts

It took years for me to believe in my dreams, visions, and intuition. Pierre played a huge role in helping me to understand the importance of being intuitive and paying attention to the guidance that comes from within. With him in the household I suddenly began to notice more things and my awareness began to increase dramatically. My relationship with Pierre was also the beginning of my having total faith in my dreams and their importance.

When our children were teenagers, I had a haunting, recurring dream three nights in a row. In this dream a huge truck was bearing down on Hazel as she rode her bike on the highway's edge. She wavered out onto the road and the driver was about to hit her when I awoke, drenched in sweat. This powerful dream was greatly disturbing and I did not know what to make of it. I had been raised Lutheran, then converted to Catholicism when I married, and yet I had other beliefs - things I could not ignore, like vivid dreams, visions, communications with spirits, guides, angels, and many other experiences that made me question being "in the box" with any religion. I found organized religion to be too oppressive, especially since I saw other things in other ways than most of the people I interacted with. I didn't realize the full significance of it then but I was in the midst of a major growth spurt.

During the period of my life when I was having that recurring nightmare I had already been struggling with my belief system. I was beginning to see that life is like a giant wheel and that there is beauty to be found in all spokes of the wheel. For example, there is beauty to be found in every religion. People often believe what they have been taught and beliefs will differ, depending upon where we were born and what culture we were raised in. The religions I knew did not emphasize intuition, intuitive visions or the importance of dream messages, and when I told Joe about this particular disturbing dream, he insisted that "no one can predict the future," so I let it go. Neither of us could guess at that time that his mind would soon be changed about the matter.

I did not yet realize what a gift it is to be strongly intuitive. And because the dream was so frightening, I did not want to believe it could be a vision of something that might actually happen.

A Dream Comes True

One day I was driving into town when I came upon the same hill that had been in that recurring nightmare. Hazel was pedaling vigorously on her bicycle toward me, just appearing over the hill. Before I even saw the truck coming up from behind her, I knew what was going to happen, and that the truck was there. Immediately, I pulled out of my lane and onto the side of the highway, almost going into the ditch. The driver of the truck managed to miss my daughter because he was able to swing around her and into my lane just in time. But the only reason I was not in his way was because that recurring dream had alerted me to what was going to happen!

I believe I saved my daughter's life that day. Since then, I have not doubted the importance of trusting my psychic intuition as well as the knowledge gained from my dreams. Both Hazel and Joe were catalysts for my change and growth that day, each of them in a different way. It was not easy for me to challenge my husband's practical doubt, but when our daughter's life was on the line, I did it in an instant.

A Gift from the Sea

My husband Joe and I have been married now for thirty-nine years. We believe it is important to stay true to oneself and to believe in one's own gifts. We have grown together over the years because we are able to give each other space to be ourselves and because of our mutual respect for one another. Even so, my intuitive gifts were challenged from time to time by my husband, especially in the beginning when I first began to pay close attention to such things. One example of this happened when we were visiting Sanibel Island, Florida.

Our trips to Florida to visit family have included some of the happiest moments of my life. Sanibel Island was like a little piece of heaven and we loved it there, especially because at that time it had not yet become popular with tourists and thus it was much more private in those days than it is now.

Usually, Joe could not get away from our family-owned grocery store to accompany the kids and me to Florida so I would go with my mom, brother, sister, and their families. Some of my favorite uncles and aunts would also meet us there, coming from various parts of the country to join the fun. On this particular year, however, Joe was able to come with us and I was ecstatic, thinking how wonderful it would be to include him in our family trip.

My husband and I both love the outdoors and some time ago we discovered the enjoyable hobby of shelling. There is a shell called a Junonia, a beautiful brown and white dotted seashell that is quite unusual and rare. It would be a remarkable addition to our collection if we could find one. So Joe offered me a challenge while we were on this trip. He challenged me to dream about a Junonia shell and to envision where we could find it.

The next night I dreamed I saw a star shining in the woods and I knew that no one else could see it but me. Then, in a second dream I saw an area with cliffs all around and a Junonia shell shining brightly on the side of the cliff. The dream felt incredibly real to me, even though cliffs seemed unlikely on Sanibel where the whole island is just a little bit above sea level. Knowing it sounded rather impossible, I remained true to my vision and told Joe about it the following morning.

A Small Miracle

Later that day, Joe went for a walk and became curious when he heard machine engines running. After some investigation, he found there was some excavating going on in a wildlife refuge. In order to create a large pond, dirt had been excavated and piled into high cliffs.

When he returned from the nature center, Joe insisted I come back there with him but did not tell me why. Down the trail we went, and when we came around the corner of a small tropical forest, there they were - the cliffs, just like in my dream!

"Is this it?" Joe asked.

"Yes, yes!" I replied, excitedly. As I walked along the side of the makeshift cliffs, I prayed, "Please God, let Joe find the shell of my vision. I have found so many shells here on the island; let him find his Junonia. It would be so special for him."

God really does hear our prayers and often answers come quickly. It was only a few minutes later that Joe called out to me in amazement.

"I found one! I found a Junonia!"

"You did?" I rushed over to him, delighted, my heart pounding with joy over this miraculous chain of events. Sure enough, there was a Junonia shell right there in his hand, and my dream vision had led us straight to it. That night, Joe and I sat and talked for hours about this experience while we celebrated with pink champagne.

An important part of this story is about giving and about having faith in your partner in life. Although my husband challenged me, he also believed in me when I confided in him and actually helped to prove the accuracy of my dream. However, the Junonia shell could still have been missed had not Joe been following his own giving nature. It just so happened that before finding that treasured shell, he had seen a perfectly shaped Conch shell, which he thought would be just the thing to bring back to our sister-in-law. She was not a habitual sheller like we were, but had been looking around for a Conch shell anyway, having decided she wanted one. So of course Joe thought of her when he saw it, and as he reached down to pick it up for her, he discovered the tip of a Junonia underneath the Conch in the sand.

So, Joe found his prized Junonia because of his generous thoughts and because of his support for my visions. Also my dream was validated, thus strengthening my belief system. We were truly led that day. It really is true: when you help others, good comes back to you and you are blessed in return.

Joe and Karla by the Sea

2
A "Meant to Be" Christmas Cat

Pierre's Philosophy

When I was a young kitten, I lived in a cattery. Karla's friend raised many cats and was especially partial to Birman felines. French Birman cats are a very sweet, wise and ancient breed known as the sacred cats of Burma – and rightfully so! According to legend, Birman cats carry the souls of priests to heaven. Before I even heard this story though, I knew my breed was a special one.

When my first caretaker discovered that I was not a good cat for show (remember my gray stocking?) she decided to sell me. First, she had me neutered, whatever that means. I think it has something to do with sex but I have no idea what that is, either. All I know is that I had what humans call a 'procedure' done and then I felt a bit tired and sore for a few days. But I also felt more peaceful, too, so I did not mind.

Some cats love to be in shows but I was secretly glad when I found out I was not going to be living that kind of a life. I preferred the idea of living with a quiet family who would love me for who I was, gray stocking and all.

It was in December of 1983 when I first saw Karla again. Of course, she had no idea that we already knew each other. She did not know that this Birman cat named Pierre was the same soul who once meowed bravely from beneath the seat of her husband's van so long before. But I knew, and I also understood that I was destined to be with Karla and her family again.

Now I have always been an easygoing, relaxed cat with a very mellow disposition. I love absolutely and unconditionally, and I enjoy wrapping my arms around my pet mom's neck to show her how much I care. However, when she first met me as Pierre, she did not realize who it was she was looking at and I had to make a great effort to make sure she picked me, bonded with me and wanted to keep me. I tried to give her strong hints so that she would recognize her old friend. I purred loudly as she held me and wrapped my paws around her wrist just like I used to when my name was Cotton. I did everything I could do to impress her with my charm. I butted the side of her head with my own the way I did in my last life as if to say, "remember me?"

I wished I had a French beret to put on as I winked at her but it didn't seem to matter that I couldn't tell her who I was, because she responded immediately to my grand gestures. Maybe she was not conscious of our past connection yet, but she adored me right from the start, so at some level she must have known.

It seemed so easy at that point but things do not always go the way we think they will. It so happened that Joe had long said he did not want an indoor cat. Karla knew a Birman cat would have to live indoors with the family but unfortunately she had promised her husband that she would never keep an indoor cat. Such a foolish promise! How would I get past this obstacle? It seemed my plan to reunite with Karla was going to be more difficult than I first imagined.

As it happened, the universe took care of things in its own way and time. When Karla reluctantly let go of me, thinking of her promise to Joe, Fate stepped in and helped to set things right. Because of this, both Karla and I would always know that being together again was indeed our destiny.

Part of the Plan

Imagine my surprise when, instead of going home with Karla, I was whisked away to join a family with young children who lived in an apartment. This was not what I had in mind at all! Some cats like a lot of noise and commotion but I found my time with that family to be disruptive and unsettling. I prefer a quieter household. As it turned out, the apartment manager informed the family that they could not keep me so back to Karla's friend I went. What a relief it was! But I was still concerned about my future; I just *had* to get back to Karla somehow.

But I needn't have worried. Destiny has its own power and I did not really have to do anything about it at all. Apparently, when Karla found out I had been returned, she was able to convince Joe to give me a chance. So, two weeks before Christmas I arrived at the household just in time for the holidays!

There I was, a happy little kitten sitting under a ten-foot high pine tree in the middle of the living room, looking up at all the fun decorations just waiting to be played with. How funny humans are, I thought. They actually dragged this huge tree inside the house, covered it with all sorts of bright, twinkling objects, and best of all, they set it in a stand that held water in it, which made a fine drinking dish for me. I tried to climb the tree once but was reprimanded for that so I didn't do it again. I don't know why such a thing should bother them but humans are funny creatures sometimes. Don't they know that climbing trees is a very cat-like thing to do?

I did get a bit of sap stuck in my long white fur, though, so maybe they had a point. It was hard to lick off so my pet mom washed my fur with a warm cloth and used a comb to get the last bits out. I noticed she was smiling as she did this, even though I had apparently misbehaved. One thing about my pet mom is that she can never stay angry with anyone for very long, and especially not with me. I have to say, I managed to get away with a lot of things over the years and I think my mischievous side even gave my pet mom a good chuckle now and then.

The family seemed to have an extra joy gene of happiness in them, which was one reason I enjoyed them so much. They are all positive thinkers and are usually happy like I am. They are even happy when there isn't any special reason to be – especially my pet mom. I understand this about her because I am the same way. The two of us are certainly kindred spirits.

That was a very satisfying Christmas for me as I acquainted myself with my new home. It was such fun to be an indoor cat! I enjoyed swatting at the decorations on the tree, and one time I managed to dislodge a silver ball so I could chase it around the living room.

As time went on, this family and I found many ways to enjoy ourselves. My pet mom and her teenagers liked to play hide and seek with me – one of my favorite games! We raced back and forth between the rooms and sometimes my pet mom would get down on her hands and knees to play with me on the floor.

When I was Cotton, I bonded more with the two older children, Caroline and Forrest. Caroline had been eleven years old when I knew her last but now she was nineteen and away at college. Forrest, who was also away at college, got to know me when he came home for visits, but now as Pierre, I was spending much more time with the younger two children, Hazel and Eric. Hazel, especially, spent a lot of time with me. She often studied and played music in her room, and I hung out with her for hours at a time, listening to Duran Duran and Rick Springfield.

When I lived as Cotton, I could not influence my pet mom as much as I wanted to because I did not live with her in the house and could not spend the time with her that I needed to in order to teach her things. But now I was an indoor cat and was free to do the job I had come to do. I set about my task, which was to teach my pet mom about animals and about our importance in the world. She began to find more and more time for me as the years went on and as I wiggled my way firmly into her heart.

People often think they do not need a pet. Then sometimes, an animal will somehow make its way into their lives and suddenly things are topsy-turvy for a while. There is an adjustment period, of course, but then these people begin to realize that bonding with pets is one of the best things that could ever happen to them. When we choose to live with humans, they should accept our decision. Humans should never give us to a shelter because they consider us a problem or because their new apartment does not accept pets.

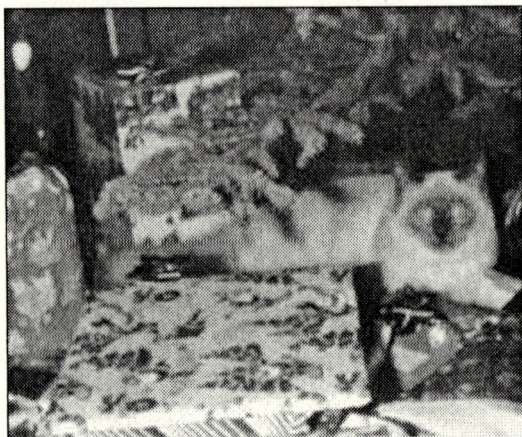

Pierre and the Christmas Presents

Pierre admiring the Christmas Tree

Send us to obedience training or find an apartment that accepts us, but don't just abandon us. There are always reasons and lessons to learn when we decide to live with someone. We animals are communicators and wish to bring messages, so give us a chance.

Karla's Celestial Thoughts

I think we all have free choices but it does seem like some things in life are predestined. When I was young, we lived in Minneapolis but my dad found property north of the Twin Cities where he designed and built a lake cottage for our family. He was a carpenter and later became an architect. He was born in Sweden and came to the United States as an immigrant when he was only nine years old. I was young when we had this cabin built, and some of my most intense and meaningful memories are from when we were out at the lake cottage in the summer months.

I used to fish with my dad at an old fishing hole, which was a very special spot in our little bay. It turned out that this was the same spot where Joe, my future husband, also liked to fish with the owner of the property in front of this place.

Although I did not know him then, all of the stars in the universe were becoming aligned. No one in my family knew it but my dad was first in line to buy the property in front of this old fishing hole if the owner ever wanted to sell it.

The twists and turns of life are often part of a grand celestial plan we do not understand. How did Dad know way back then how important it would be for him to buy this land? He had the foresight to realize there was so much more to this old fishing haunt than met the eye. Years later it would happen that Joe also wanted this property, and just before we got married he tried to purchase it. However, when he talked to the previous owner, the man told Joe he was sorry but he had already sold it to someone else. The 'someone else', of course, turned out to be my father. It was fate at the old fishing hole, as this lake and place spun its magic on two souls destined to be connected someday. So when Dad surprised us at our engagement party and gave Joe and me this property for a wedding gift, it did seem to be destiny.

Fateful Date with the Full Moon

He owned a family grocery store and ran it with his dad.
I never thought he noticed me, but later found he had.
That summer when I noticed him, our family was at our cabin.
I never thought we might go out - that it could ever happen.

My family bought our groceries there, and Joe was fun to see.
Each time I shopped for groceries, somehow he would wait on me.
We had a summer cabin, which was by this same small town,
So, I saw him in the grocery store, as he was always around.

One Friday night, the moon was full, as I ascended the back steps.
He stood there gazing at the moon, and I will never forget.
The world seemed soft and mystical, all blanketed in light.
The earth stood still, as we both talked on that ethereal night

He took a break from working and it seemed like this was fate.
We talked about so many things, and I asked him for a date.
Life's timing really means so much, and people's circumstance.
We were meant to talk that fateful night - it really was not chance.

I could not understand why all of my feelings ran so deep,
But when I saw him on those stairs, my soul within me leaped.
The moment was so powerful, as I joined him on the stairs.
I had to talk to him that night - I took a chance and dared.

He had just made the decision - he was going to leave the store.
He was moving to Alaska, which he wanted to explore.
Later I discovered why I must see him that night.
I had simply felt the urgency, and now know I was right.

It was true that he was leaving, but that decision changed.
He was moving to Alaska, but his life was rearranged.
Later, I felt that moonlit night was surely meant to be
That somehow we are soul mates, throughout all eternity.

The chemistry is there, or not - you feel it in your soul.
It is something you cannot explain, something you just know.
I felt like I was coming "home" - I felt such happiness.
I dated other men in life, but never felt like this.

Our meeting underneath the moon was in a grand celestial plan.
We were meant to be together - I was meant to know this man.
As we stood there underneath the moon with that soft summer breeze,
The angels guided us as we both changed our destinies.

Opposites Attract

Our religions are quite different and our ages far apart.
I knew it would not matter, and I felt that from the start.
We are such total opposites, me so messy, him so neat.
Yet we both are still together - it is an amazing feat.

We married and I always know he will be my true love.
I am so very grateful to the angels from above.
He is calm, I am excitable - he is private and I socialize.
I like junk food; he likes health food,
yet somehow our lives do harmonize.

He always has been orderly and logical I know.
All things are either black or white; he clearly thinks it so.
I have found in life's experiences, this I would never say.
So many things that I have seen are more a muted gray.
I am into things artistic and creative ways pursue.

I often like to try new ways to keep my life renewed.
I am Pisces, he is Virgo - we are many poles apart.
Still it does not really matter, as we both share one big heart.

He does not always understand me or my psychic ways, I know.
That doesn't matter either - sensitivity he shows.
We sometimes have had storms, which both of us have weathered.
We both have flaws, like everyone -
yet through them we grew together.

We could not be more different, yet the two of us don't care.
He is up early, I'm a night owl, but the middle hours we share.
Joe likes pop and I like opera, so our tastes do not agree.
He likes sports, I like old movies, yet we live in harmony.

I was raised in the Twin Cities, yet adjusted to his country life.
In fact I now prefer it, and I see it in another light.
Though there are many differences - when you review the facts,
It is unexplainable, but love is attainable - opposites attract.

Special Communication

Being married and raising four children kept me very busy, but
I did take the time to explore many other interests. One of these was
watercolor painting, and I took some lessons at one time from an
instructor who had a cockatoo, a beautiful bird, which I admired a
great deal. One day when I came in for my usual lesson, the cockatoo
was not in its cage. My instructor was a bit concerned that I might not
care for this distraction.

"Does it bother you to have him flying around?"

"No," I said, quickly. "I love animals. I love creatures of every
kind."

So she left him out as we began our work and soon he swept down
to the table near me. I smiled as he crept slowly up to me, and then
smiled wider as he became even braver and climbed up my arm. Soon
he was sitting on my shoulder, cooing at me. I had to laugh, it was
so funny, and I think my painting began to improve the moment he
touched me. I believe animals often help people to be more creative. I

was delighted to find that beautiful cockatoo out of his cage that day, especially when he climbed up my arm to help me!

"What would you like to paint now?" my instructor asked, thinking it was time to do more than just go over painting techniques. I thought for a moment, then said,

"Angels."

So, with this marvelous creature sitting on my shoulder, I created my first painting of the angel Joyelle, who is one of my guides. It seemed perfect timing, the way it all came together that special day.

I believe we constantly receive messages from Spirit and nature. Sometimes, it takes us a while to understand these connections but we should always look for them. They are everywhere!

3

Metaphysical Cat & Metaphysical Pet Mom

Pierre's Philosophy

I have shared many of the same experiences my pet mom has had as a psychic throughout the centuries. Years ago, cats were persecuted and tortured for being intuitive and metaphysical "witches." This is ridiculous; we are highly evolved, but good creatures in the world. The Egyptians loved, honored and appreciated us because they understood our value. My pet mom dreamed of a life with me in Egypt and felt we were truly there together. She believes that is where she first met me. In this lifetime I feel things, mystical things. I am most happy to be a cat.

Cats stretch and understand instinctively the concepts of yoga as it comes naturally for us. We believe in living in the moment, enjoying life now, and always counting our blessings. Cats are resilient, having nine lives. We often go through many difficult times but always with great dignity and grace. We have courage.

A Magical Experience

When I was just a kitten, my pet mom had an astral travel experience that helped her to realize just how special I was and how important I would be to her. At that time, her teenagers were often going in and out of the house at various times so she put me into an extra large animal cage at night so I wouldn't be able to slip outside if someone happened to leave the door open.

My pet dad was always the first one up in the morning so he would let me out of my night quarters. Immediately, I would race into the master bedroom and jump onto the bed where I could pounce around my pet mom's feet. It was a great game. She would awaken and pick me up, cuddle and love me. She often talked in a babbling, endearing language, as only humans can do when they love someone dearly.

One day she woke up to find me bouncing around on her bed as usual, so she laughed and sat up, reaching to pet me, but suddenly could not find me. Where was I? My pet dad had forgotten to let me out that morning because he was late for work and in a hurry. I concentrated as I sat in my cage, and zoom, I was out of my body and astral traveling to her room playing my usual little game with her. Boy, was she surprised when she looked down to find me and I was not there!

She was very puzzled, but not too startled as she intuitively realized I must still be in my cage. I had astral traveled. So as she arose and went to open my cage, I flipped back into my body waiting for her to come. It is normal for my pet mom to have spirits visit her. Still, I don't think she ever had a pet do this before; the experience awakened my pet mom to a lot of other possibilities.

Though it may seem that cats sometimes stare at nothing for hours, we may actually be seeing spirits or we may be seeing and communicating on other levels. We are very busy with our own introspective, spiritual life.

Have you ever noticed how many cats hang out in bookstores? That is because we are intellectual and are always thinking about things. Our minds are always in a whirl. We threaten people sometimes with our depth of perception and heightened awareness. We cannot be fooled. We are tremendous communicators, as was demonstrated by my astral traveling to see my pet mom. Cats can teach people to appreciate unusual communication by using their own intuition. This comes naturally to us. Being intuitive is simply a matter of trusting your inner knowledge.

Karla's Celestial Thoughts

I learned about astral travel years ago while taking intuitive classes with Mary, a well-known hypnotist and psychic reader in Minneapolis. She turned out to be a good friend and mentor. This older woman, who was short in stature with blond hair and twinkling blue eyes, radiated love. I studied with her for three years.

I went to Mary for the purpose of recalling a past life, although at the time I was wondering if reincarnation was real. Mary had me lie down on a bed to relax and then helped me to reach a meditative state. She later told me I was a natural student. I was thrilled to know that all of my time spent learning how to meditate had paid off! I had practiced many types of meditation over the years so that I could delve into the spiritual realms much more deeply. Much of being intuitive is simply practice, practice, practice. Everyone is intuitive, but some of us use or practice it much more than others.

Karla meditating with candles

Visiting the Past

Mary helped me to regress into three lifetimes that day but the most important one was as a gypsy in Europe, where I had cards I used for readings. When Mary asked me about these cards, I said they were my own and that someday I would create them again in this lifetime. I had completely forgotten this particular statement of mine until recently. It wasn't until I listened to the tape of that session again, for the purpose of recalling events for this book, that I remembered what I had said about recreating those cards.

Mary also brought me back to my early childhood and asked why I came into this lifetime. I immediately told her that it was so I could teach my parents and siblings about being different, being psychic, and how it is okay to be intuitive and seemingly different. I think we all come into certain families to teach lessons and to learn from each other, and that often we come in clusters or groups, from life to life, in order to learn these lessons and to go further along the path to spirituality.

Many of the religions in the world believe in reincarnation, and I know I do because of my own experiences. Some of my clients in my intuitive readings tell me they do not believe they would ever come into the families they are in. However, I think they did choose this life for whatever reason. A person can be a man in one life, a woman in another, rich in one, poor in another, gay or straight, black or white. A son could be a mother or a father could be a daughter, etc.

Navigating by Intuition

Mary talked a lot about astral travel. She suggested trying it in the middle of the night or during the early morning hours when sleepy and half awake, because a person is more receptive then. One night I awakened in the middle of the night and decided to try to astral travel out to Richfield to the old house where I grew up. My dad had died years before but my mother had just passed away about a month before this incident happened.

My brother had a friend named Guy who was staying at our home in Richfield for personal reasons while we tried to sell it. I had forgotten he was living there. It turned out that he had been visiting someone else overnight on the night I had this experience.

I was out of my body quickly, up to the ceiling and moving swiftly through the darkened sky. It all happened so fast. First I felt I was traveling over the land. Then I wanted to go down to my mother's old house. I went right through the front door of her house, down the hall, and landed on my feet, standing shakily while gazing into the bathroom. There was my mother, appearing as a bright blue ethereal light in the bathroom. She turned to me, appearing a bit confused as she looked around our old bathroom. There were wet towels all over the place, on the curtain rack, the sink and the bathtub rim, on hooks by the door and on towel racks. It looked very cluttered and odd, and although I knew I was dreaming, it all seemed so real.

I felt this was a fragile moment so I yelled at Mom in order to get her attention, telling her our girls were taking ballet lessons like she had wanted them to. She turned, looked at me directly, and smiled. I was touched and delighted to see her again and to know she was all right. It was a dramatic and overwhelmingly happy moment for me.

Meditating with Crystals

Proof in the Real World

After that, I was rushing through the air again at a tremendous rate and I snapped back into my body from the top of my head and awakened with a jolt. I prayed to God and the angels that I would have some kind of affirmation that I really did astral travel and this was not just a dream.

The next day I had lunch with my brother, which was a rare occasion as we hardly ever have the opportunity to get together. As I was telling him about this dream, he suddenly turned white and said, "Oh my God, you were there." It turned out he had been out to Richfield just that morning, finding the basement flooded and towels strewn all over the bathroom which Guy had placed there to dry. I was so excited! It was not just a dream. I was really there, and it proved to me that this truly had happened!

We can listen to our 'gut feelings' in life and learn to trust our inner knowledge. Dreams can often show us what we really feel and what is truly going on, with symbolism and metaphors. Astral traveling can teach us many things and can bring us new knowledge about other worlds.

Rediscovering past lives can help us realize why we have certain gifts or interests in life, or certain fears, or why we really like or dislike some people - what they were to us in a past life and how we can change a relationship in this life or learn a certain lesson.

Order of Melchizedek, Another Dream

Three years ago in May, I had a dream which was also to be very significant in my life. In this dream I was in Egypt where I saw a symbol in the sand of a triangle, a line and a circle, all on top of each other. The rest of that week I kept doodling the symbol over and over. One day while at work I was drawing it again when a friend noticed what I was doing and asked about it.

"I don't know what it is," I told her, "but it has shown up in my dreams three times so far. It has to mean something."

"It does mean something," she exclaimed, suddenly very excited, and went on to explain that this particular symbol represented a ministry called the Order of Melchizedek.

"Reverend Dan from the Order of Melchizedek flies all over the country ordaining people into the priesthood," she said. "and guess what… he's going to be here in Minnesota next week!"

Of course, I felt the timing of it all was amazing so I went ahead and went through the process of training to become a minister in this Order.

At the first class, Reverend Dan asked all twenty of us how we had come to do this. To my astonishment, we all said the same thing: that we had a dream or a vision or were otherwise mysteriously led to come to this place in order to be ordained. Reverend Dan said everyone who came to him seemed to have a deep need to help humanity, and he felt they had done this in other lives also. During the ceremony (which I chose to go through by myself without family) when they gave me a staff and anointed me with oils and used crystals on the altar, I felt myself spinning into other lives while simultaneously trying to remain grounded here on earth and maintain focus on the ceremony.

It was an overwhelmingly beautiful experience, which I feel was "meant to be." Dreams truly do lead us, and to be metaphysical simply means to follow one's inner knowledge.

Meditating with Caroline

4

Apples & Oranges: Different Kinds of Friends

Joe with the kids and a new friend

Pierre's Philosophy

Dozer was an outdoor dog, a black lab who was a wonderful pet for the family. I never quite understood him, though. I would sit at the window and watch Dozer charging around outdoors with his usual exuberance and couldn't help but think he seemed a bit too enthusiastic. One day I decided to visit him in the astral world while he was taking a nap in his dog pen outside.

He was really a nice sort for a dog but I was careful in how I approached him, because I certainly didn't want to startle him as I reached into his doggie dream. I knew he was dreaming because whenever Dozer was in dreamland he twitched his tail and seemed to smile in his sleep.

I told him that I was the family's indoor cat. Although we had never met before, I wanted to talk to him to see what he was all about. He seemed to want to communicate also, curious about my role in this family.

Different Strokes

Dozer said he liked to make our pet parents happy. He was loving and devoted to the family, aiming to please. I told him that I would rather appear independent, stately and decorative, although of course I really wanted to be loved also. I just did not want to be obvious about it.

I like to spend hours grooming myself and grooming our pet mom's face, if she lets me. Dozer would rather run through the swamp and mud puddles, get dirty digging up bones and charge around playing fetch with a stick. He was the rough and tough type of creature.

I am fastidious and like certain kinds of cat foods and treats. I really like cheese, being a French Birman cat. Dozer thought this was ridiculous and liked everything edible, and some things not edible. He liked chewing on things, anything, really. Heavens, how disgusting!

Dozer said he liked to be needed and liked to help our pet dad with his pheasant hunting. He felt he was doing something useful but I told him I would rather simply love these people and feel useful by just being there. Not that I just sit on pillows and eat bonbons!

Over the years I have killed three mice families. We all have our own instincts and I do hunt at times, with no apologies for being a cat. It is in my genes and make up to do this and I have pride in my accomplishments.

Dozer wondered how cats can nap so much when there are things to dig up and investigate. (I decided at this point that I should not remind him that our visit was taking place while he was taking his nap, right then). I told him I do investigate but do it spiritually in my mind, going to other dimensions with my soul. I am really very busy when I take naps.

It was nice to know we were both doing the jobs which we were assigned to do on earth - helping humans and being there for them. I also told Dozer about Prince the tree frog that Hazel had in her room, and how Prince would make peeping noises sometimes in his terrarium. Dozer thought this was amusing but he could not understand why any creature would make such noises when all they had to do was bark loudly like he did.

I feel Dozer had a lot of wisdom in him - knowing when to come bounding up to the humans and when to just be there with them, and how to bond with them. My conclusion as I said good-bye to him, was that we all have our own jobs to do and our own unique ways of doing them.

Dozer and Joe,
the hunters

Clearing the Way

Snagglepuss was a tough, feisty, tiger striped cat that was already living at the house when I arrived. During the cold winter months, Eric sometimes let Snagglepuss into the house to warm up for a while. I am not sure the rest of the family knew he let him in. Snagglepuss had a carpet lined, double layered cathouse made with layers of straw placed for warmth above the carpet. He had water and food at all times and seemed very hearty, but liked to come into the house at night once in a while.

Snagglepuss wanted to be petted only on his own terms and when he had had enough, he would turn around and bite whoever was petting him. He was like some humans who can seem caustic and yet have hearts of gold. One night when he was in the house, he passed me on the staircase. Eric had tried to keep Snagglepuss downstairs, separated from me since I was upstairs, but actually Snagglepuss and I did not pay attention to each other when we met.

I think the humans could have found a solution for both of us to live together eventually but the truth was that Snagglepuss would never be happy inside all of the time, and was so much more of a wild country cat. He liked to tomcat around and run in the woods and the swamp. I am bred to live inside, lounging on soft pillows. I might have seemed wimpy to him if he had ever gotten to know me.

Unfortunately, one day Snagglepuss disappeared. The family couldn't find him anywhere, and although they looked down by the lake, all over in the woods and swamp, and they asked neighbors to let them know if they saw anything, they never found him again. Right about that time an owl was heard in the woods and since Snagglepuss was a small tomcat, I wonder if the owl ate him. Although I have not been exposed to them, I do know there are predators out there and difficult life styles that may cause one to be in dangerous situations. I was fortunate to never have to deal with that.

The family was very upset about Snagglepuss. I know my pet mom mourned for him, especially since she did not know where he was, and I think she felt guilty because Snagglepuss disappeared right after I arrived, but he would not want her to feel that way. That is not how the Animal Kingdom works. We don't believe in guilt. I do believe

Snagglepuss was supposed to leave this world at the time I came to earth again, as he was clearing the way for me to be in the household without any conflicts. I am grateful to him for that.

There are all kinds of creatures in life, living their own life styles, and they should not be judged for their assorted ways. We should not be prejudiced. There is so much to learn when we can appreciate our differences. Humans and animals come in many colors, sizes, and styles. I love all of them!

Karla's Celestial Thoughts

St. Fiacre, and the Seven Sisters

I have a group of friends who are perennial friends, friends for life. We call ourselves the Seven Sisters after the Pleiades constellation which is comprised of seven stars. I have known them since I was young, as they all lived close to our summer lake cottage, and the seven of us formed close bonds during our many magical summers at the lake. There are three sets of sisters and one lone woman in this "Seven Sisters Family" and although we all went off to engage in our own experiences later on, we reunited on my 50th birthday. We have enjoyed many parties and get-togethers since then, our bond as strong as ever.

I was with the youngest of the Sisters one day in a small town in Wisconsin and we were walking together past some quaint little shops when I had a flash of insight and just knew I had to go inside this one particular store.

"Will you come with me in here?" I asked, pointing to the funky little store I felt drawn towards. Even though I had never visited this particular town before, I knew there was a St. Fiacre statue in this shop. St. Fiacre is the saint of gardening and nature and I had been looking for a statue of him for about a month.

So my "little sister," who is always a good sport, accompanied me as we browsed through this place which was filled with old gold framed pictures, hanging mobiles, musty smelling old books, holiday decorations, pottery, glassware and sculptures.

"No, I don't have that specific statue," the shopkeeper told me when I asked about St. Fiacre but I knew she was wrong. For some reason, I was drawn to the back of the store where I found the back door and walked out into a small garden, and there, in an enclosed area where there were many yard ornaments, a St. Fiacre statue was waiting for me. Boy, was the shopkeeper surprised!

St. Fiacre now stands as a sentinel in our vegetable garden. When I first put him in the garden, I had to extend the garden plot as the very next day my squash had grown so much that they needed more room. All my plants experienced a tremendous growth spurt that summer as St. Fiacre spun his magic in the garden.

Karla with St. Fiacre, Saint of Gardening

Pleiades Perennials, The Seven Sisters

I have six dear, perennial friends, back from my deep past.
We all were reunited at my fiftieth birthday bash.
My sister held a party for me with these precious friends.
They are perennial treasures, and on them I can depend.

We reminisced about the past, and playing at the farm.
And also at our lake cottages, as life back then had charm.
Two Dutch, German, and Swedish sisters formed our cosmic group.
And one alone, completed our own international loop.
Our farm mother made homemade bread, which we loved to eat.
We sat around her wooden table, each with our own seat.
All kinds of plants were on her porch, an old washboard there too.
She always welcomed us with warmth, though she had work to do.

We played in the barn and silo - somewhere on the farm each day,
Swinging on twine across the loft and landing in the hay.
Playing with "cars," and paper dolls, and many kinds of cards,
and getting nervous when the bull got loose, somewhere in the yard.

I recall pigs, cows, and chickens, cats, and one lone guard dog too.
The farm seemed lots of fun, yet there were many chores to do.
Nature can seem difficult, with the realities of a farm,
and yet with some harsh truths in life, the world still has a charm.

Picking berries in summertime, we learned to work and share,
Also making money for the Fourth and the State Fair.
The glory of July Fourth was a thrill for us each year,
Carnival rides, the grand parade, the patriotic cheer.

And then to end this magical time, we saw fireworks by the lake,
As Vince, the neighbor, had his own, with which to illuminate.
Another special mom in the group, brought us to movies and shows,
This was our big entertainment, so we were always anxious to go.

We played games outside in the evenings, games which we made up,
Taking breaks by an old well, as we drank from a silver cup.
By the lake there was a single bench, set between two trees,
This was a special spot to rest, and brings back memories.

This mother had us in for popcorn, served in wooden bowls.
Her house had Indian rugs, and brightness, such a warmth and glow.
My mom served lunches on a picnic table, sandwiches of melted cheese,
As whenever our group would play together,
there were many mouths to feed.

Our fourth mother by the lake would cluck, and clean, and sweetly fuss,
Inviting us to her house also, although the place must not be mussed.
These four mothers created our childhood memories with enduring love.
I say thank you to our mothers, now in heaven up above.

As we grew older we walked, and talked, and slept with stars at night.
In the autumn, meteor showers were a most spectacular sight.
To renew these golden friendships, you can always pick up threads.
Although for years you had not heard, and nothing had been said.

Our love has turned to polished gold with friendships from the past.
Our lives are intertwined like vines, with these the ties that last.
So, these friendships are a sacred gift - their value can't be measured.
We should cultivate this garden as true friendships are a treasure.

Pennies from Heaven

I met Betsy at an intuition class and we quickly became friends. We
had a lot in common, including Indian spirit guides. She introduced me
to the Women's Spirituality Conference, which is held every autumn
in Mankato, Minnesota. The first time I spoke there in front of a group,
she was my assistant. Sadly, I only had her in my life for about five
years because after a brave struggle she eventually succumbed to
cancer and died. I will always remember her courage. Before she
passed away, however, Betsy promised she would bring me messages
from the afterlife.

She did not tell me these messages would come in the form of
pennies, although I should have guessed. The night before that first
conference we stayed at a convent that had rooms open to the public
and we were talking to each other as we lay in our twin beds. I had just
said I hoped the spirits were going to help us the next day when I was
to speak about the animal/people connection. She agreed, and right
at that instant we heard something go flying across the room from in
between us by the night stand.

I got up to solve the mystery but the only thing I found was a
penny on the floor. I picked it up and handed it to Betsy.

"You are my lucky penny." I told her, smiling.

After she died, time passed and I completely forgot about her promise to send me a message. It was funny I didn't think of it when I kept finding pennies in so many places, particularly when I went back yearly to the spirituality conference and when I was working on my writing. Betsy had always encouraged my writing and wanted me to finish my books.

There were other "penny" references, too. In one of my animal/people connection classes in Mankato there was a woman who wanted to talk about her dog who had died. She thought this dog was an angel dog, and had named her Penny. Another year, I had a woman who desperately wanted an intuitive reading so I gave her an hour reading at my booth before I was to give my talk. Her name was Penny. Then, I found pennies in the bathroom, in the parking lot and the halls. But even with all that, I did not get the connection of these messages from Betsy.

It finally leapt into my awareness one day when I went to a fast food restaurant to bring home dinner. I didn't want to spend time cooking that day because I wanted to write instead, something Betsy would have understood. After I picked up the food and returned to the car, I looked down to find six pennies by the car door. I knew they hadn't been there when I walked into the restaurant. I began picking them up when all of a sudden I realized what had been happening over and over: Betsy was sending me messages! Chills flowed from my hand, up my arm and through my entire body. There were six pennies on the ground and Betsy was trying to tell me to use my sixth sense! I connected all of this and realized she had been trying to reach me in spirit for a long time. Friendships go far beyond the grave. Animal connections do too, as when a pet may visit us after dying. Spirit does indeed live forever.

Other Friends

Another friend of mine loves islands as do I, and I think we knew each other in a past life on an island somewhere. In this life we have traveled together to Anna Maria Island, Florida, Madeline Island, Wisconsin, and Kauai, Hawaii - experiences I will never forget. In Kauai, we were seated at an Irish restaurant on St. Patrick's day, talking about our mothers and their connections. My friend's mother had died on this day years ago and I had been thinking about my own mother also, remembering my life with her. It had sometimes been difficult as she had not always been nurturing but as I was sitting there in the middle of this restaurant, all of a sudden I felt my mother's spirit around me. I received a healing from her at that moment.

I also have a Lone Star friend from Texas, very feisty and rambunctious but caring and very courageous, too. She lost her husband a few years ago and since she was despondent after his death, she asked Spirit for a sign that he was still around her. Someone had given her a huge plant after the funeral and soon after she discovered there were Forget-Me-Not flowers sprouting from underneath the leaves of this plant. Nobody knew these flowers were with the plant, not even the greenhouse that had sold it in the first place. She was comforted, knowing that the flowers were a message from her dead husband.

Another friend of mine who is very intuitive sometimes tunes into visions which I have had. Years ago I was in Trinidad, California visiting my daughter Caroline and walking along the seashore. I decided to rest on a sand dune and gaze at the ocean. As I was meditating, I looked up and saw three angels, pink, purple and green, standing above a sand dune in a vision in the sky, bringing me a message of love. This was on my birthday and I was far from home, so it was such a wonderful experience to be visited by angels. When I returned to Minnesota, this intuitive friend of mine gave me a watercolor painting. It had three angels on it wearing pink, purple and green dresses, respectively. I was startled at the way she so accurately depicted these spirits.

Years ago, I knew an elderly woman named Lee who lived in the north woods. She loved animals and taught me a lot about them, and about nature. She showed me how to blend in with animals in their habitat so they would not have to adjust to us. Lee had squirrels who raced around her legs and chipmunks who climbed up her body and raided her pockets, knowing they would find peanuts there. She even fed a bear who appeared in her yard every night. However, one of her lessons to me was to be aware of stepping over boundaries. When she left her cabin in the fall, the bear she had fed daily still wanted food, having learned to depend on her too much. One night, the bear tore into her porch when she was not home and destroyed her property.

One can learn many things from friends, and from Lee I learned not only that a connection with wild animals can be rewarding but also that one should not foster dependence of a wild animal.

Spirits Coming In

I was on vacation with my husband and a couple of our friends with whom we have a lot of family history. Joe and his pal were out fishing and Marie and I were commiserating in the living room of our cabin. She was smoking a cigarette and we had just eaten some soup in the kitchen which I had heated up on our old cook stove. We laughed about trying to be like pioneers with this old equipment in the cabin. We were each resting on bunk beds in the living room when suddenly the smoke from the kitchen floated into the room and hovered over my bed.

At this point I had been developing my psychic awareness for quite a few years so nothing shocked me anymore, but Marie was surprised and uneasy.

"Don't be nervous," I told her. "It's just a guide."

She said, "Oh yeah?" and took a huge gulp as she stared at this whirlwind of smoke now spinning in large circles over my bed. I knew it was her Aunt Lacey Mae, whom I found out later had died. She was okay on the "other side," and wanted to tell my friend this. Just as I figured this out, the smoke pulled itself together in a small ball and went whissssh, right out of the closed window of the cabin.

Often spirits will use a source like cigarette smoke or the smoke from a wood stove and enhance it, working with the energies of it. Marie then began to believe in ghosts and spirits and no longer doubted me. That is usually what it takes - a personal experience for someone to realize there are ghosts and spirits in the world.

Two Feathers

One day another friend, Bright Star, came to visit me. She was teaching me Reiki and we had developed a very good friendship, sharing many things. As we sat in our kitchen talking, I had a sudden, strong feeling we should walk down to the lake. I listened to my intuition and led my friend down to the shoreline. When we reached the lake, a majestic eagle swept in and circled us, then flew up into an ash tree to join a second eagle!

From this tree, about 20 feet away, they sat gazing at us with wise eyes, seemingly unafraid of our close proximity. We shared a very powerful moment with these regal birds. They brought us a message of freedom and openness to higher truths, encouraging us to discover a higher purpose together.

Won't You Be My Neighbor?

Our neighbors, two women, became very good friends with us. They arrived next door bringing dogs, cats, bird feeders, flowers, friendliness, smiles, helpfulness and very good vibrations. When they first met me I was racing across their yard to take a picture of a sunset from their property where I could view it better from the lake. They later told me that they were a bit surprised to see a tall, gangly woman with a funny purple, floppy hat and old baggy pants and shirt running across their yard to catch a picture of the final rays of the sun.

They did not laugh at me when I put wet clothes on the line after dark or when I cut the lawn with yard lights on at night or when I had lanterns by my side at night when I started digging our vegetable garden as I did not have time in the day. They began to realize I was rather nocturnal and also a bit unusual.

They helped one of our sons get out of the ditch one weekend when his car went off the road, gave me tea and vitamins when I had the flu and lent me eggs and coffee. One of them has such a kind heart she once put an umbrella over her petunias as they were getting too much sun. These ladies took Streak, our Springer, for a pontoon ride on a weekend when they were dog-sitting for him and they were sweet enough to put up an electric fence when their black Chow was having a boundary conflict with Joe.

After we shared the death of a mutual friend, we became even closer. I felt I understood them a lot better and truly discovered what kind and wonderful neighbors they are. We are blessed to have neighbors who are also good friends.

The Old Country

Another lesson one of my friends taught me was about being authentic. Just imagine: after you walk up the stone steps to her quaint little house, you step over the threshold into another world, surrounded by the cozy feeling of the old country. In her warm, friendly kitchen she has the aroma of baked bread and spices and she welcomes you with open arms and a thick Italian accent. Smiling, with warm brown eyes, she graciously asks you to sit down. You gaze around at the beautifully carved religious statues, rosaries and crosses, and breathe in the scent of flowers in every room. You feel the faith of this woman and you forget you are in America as you seem to spin into another place, another time. Surely this is old Europe, you think. A time of grace and beauty.

This lovely host serves fragrant coffee and stirs up memories of a simpler time. She always wears natural fabrics and she herself is very real, in no way synthetic. You feel you are blessed to know her and her attitudes of honesty, acceptance, joy and love. Her haven of happiness is like an oasis in the desert in these hectic times.

Art with Friends

Life has many angles - lines often are not straight.
Artists may find different ways in which they can relate.
So many things in life are art - surprising ways can be the norm.
If we will just keep open minds, true art can come in many forms

Install a window in a home, or change the plumbing in a sink,
Write a story late at night, as you ponder and you think,
Design a brand new fishing lure, or develop a new exercise,
Combine colors for a lipstick - it's an art we may not realize.

Use feng-shui techniques to change the furniture in your home,
Move rocks around a garden, making paths where one may roam.
Gather up old photographs and recreate a family's past,
As history comes together in these memories which last.

To walk on a slow treadmill, or run outdoors, a mile,
Lift weights or do karate - exercise in your own style.
Hit a golf ball with a tail spin, around a tree onto the green,
It is an art to make this shot, coming out so clean.

Shoot a basket in a hoop, or throw a graceful football pass,
Hit a cue ball with perfect spin to win a challenging game at last.
Sculpt your body with pilates, or graceful moves of Tai Chi.
Fencing, boxing, ballet steps - all are art to some degree.

Art brings one to another world, as we dance or sing.
Music is most universal, in all that's happening.
Play a sweet viola, or a jazzy saxophone,
Or a grand piano, with assorted nuances and tones.

A friend of mine in college was in many different plays,
I recall that "Little theater," where he spent many days.
He taught me to appreciate the way stories are told -
All the lessons one can learn as dramas do unfold.

Karen M. creates mosaics, from tiny bits of tile,
Making new kaleidoscopes - bright and bold and wild.
A friend has sacrificed for art, which she successfully teaches.
She has a gift with children - there are many whom she reaches.

Mary paints with watercolor, following her dreams.
Jeannie paints other universes, she feels that she has seen.
A friend brought me to operas - this is music I love best.
With all I learn from these special friends, I feel I have been blessed.

Art is very plentiful - we just need to look around,
And if we do explore things, brand new avenues are found.
Art is most empowering as you find your way.
It is vital to the universe and enriches lives each day.

Light Workers

Karen reaches for a higher purpose - following her vision.
Uniting the world in body, mind, Spirit - this is her grand mission.
She created this holistic center - people come from miles around,
a place of truth and freedom, where life's answers can be found.

People from all walks of life are welcome to this center.
A place of light and hopefulness - a haven we can enter.
These are very trying times, and people are so stressed.
This haven Karen created is a place where one can rest.

I have found my purpose also, helping others in my own way.
I know in my own life that good things happen when you pray.
To be intuitive is a gift, following your inner choices.
You are co-creating with Spirit, by discovering your inner voice.

There are so many intuitive tools, like discovering astrology,
Or automatic writing, or the truths of numerology.
So many ways to find your truths, too numerous to say,
At this holistic center, you may learn to find your way.

Acceptance is the key to life, letting people be themselves,
Awakening their consciousness - no longer sitting on some shelf.
We need to face the world with faith, we need to have great courage,
In this, a challenging universe, we shall not get discouraged.

For, angels are assisting - heavenly helpers greet us every day,
They flit around with peaceful joy, as they show the way.
We must be spiritual warriors - fighting the battle for truth and light,
Always with great courage, and a purity of purpose in our sights.

At the Metaphysical Emporium we brought together light and love,
and I believe we all are helped by angels up above.
I'm glad to be a friend of Karens, in many ways we think alike,
Besides our family and friends we love, we keep this mission in our sight.

Perennial Friends and Annual Friends

Some friends come into our lives annually - just for a brief while. Other friends are perennials - forever friends with whom we can pick up a friendship, even if we haven't seen them for years. I have many kinds of friends, human and animal, in this lifetime. I treasure all of them. True friends are a rare commodity; they have a value you cannot measure. They are the jewels in our lives.

5
Healings, Rescues, & Heart to Heart Talks

Pierre's Philosophy

I once helped a boy who was visiting us, a young teenager who was troubled. I just felt he needed some extra love and even though I am usually reluctant to walk up to strangers, he was just too distraught to ignore. He was upset about a girl friend with whom he was having problems.

I jumped up on his lap and purred and groomed him all over his face, drying his tears with my tongue. He seemed to enjoy this. I was a good diversion for him, taking his mind off of his troubles. This boy was allergic to other cats but not to me. After all, I do have an angelic vibration that cuts through barriers!

Teeny Tiny Man

Ho-Ho was a wonderful little black Pekinese who suffered from physical problems all of his life. Even though he wasn't aware of it, he had deformed legs and this made him unfit to be a show dog. Ho-Ho believed he was beautiful because his doting pet mom and dad adored him so much. He was able to read their thoughts and when his pet mom became depressed now and then, Ho-Ho stayed close by her side being as helpful as possible. Dogs read your moods and attempt to help you accordingly.

Ho-Ho died this past year but his pet parents will never forget their "little teeny tiny man." He will live forever in their hearts.

Polly, the Guide Dog

My pet mom's friend lives with Polly who is a Golden Retriever guide dog. This woman is physically disabled, but her faithful friend helps her through the many challenges of life.

Polly came from a family of 11 and almost all of her siblings are guide dogs. She helps to do laundry by carrying clothes from the dryer one article at a time. She opens doors and can pick up many things from the floor, even coins. She is always alert, watching for any possible danger nearby and cheerfully helps my pet mom's friend to cope with problems in her life.

Chester, the Cat

Another way we animals help humans is by rescuing them when they need our help. This pet story is about Lucille, a woman my pet mom met at a nursing home. While visiting her mother-in-law, my pet mom wandered down the hall to the entrance area where there was a huge aviary. Lucille was also there, watching the singing birds, and soon the two of them began to talk.

Lucille, who was 83 years old, had broken a hip. She was staying in the nursing home to recover but really missed her cat Chester and could not wait to get back home to him.

"He saved my life," she said, fondly. Then she told my pet mom the story about how she was standing on a chair in her apartment trying to change a light bulb but lost her balance and fell. Chester was so alarmed he raced to the doorway and scratched repeatedly with his paws, making high, loud screeching sounds until the superintendent of the apartment complex came to the door to see what was happening. He opened the door to discover Lucille lying there on the floor, helpless and in pain. Had it not been for Chester's efforts, Lucille could have suffered there for days, alone and frightened.

Once she was fully recovered, Lucille was planning to take Chester and move in with her daughter. Luckily, her daughter loved Chester, too. Who wouldn't love a quick-thinking, life-saving cat like that?

I was so happy when my pet mom told me this story. I love happy endings – especially for animals!

The Harp Seal of Kauai

Years ago in Hawaii, my pet mom was on a trip with a friend. She took a cruise boat up the west side of Kauai for the day but half way to their destination the boat suddenly came to a stop. The captain of the ship said they would be delayed for about half an hour because there was a harp seal on the beach that needed to be rescued. Apparently, two men were harassing the poor, frightened creature.

The humans watched from the side rail of the cruise ship as a crew member motored to shore in a small craft, surprising the men on the beach with some hefty fines. He ordered them away from the area so the vulnerable seal could rest on the beach in peace.

The humans continued on their trip with a good feeling of having helped this defenseless seal. I purred with pride when my pet mom told me this story because sometimes animals save humans, and sometimes it is the other way around. I think it is a very nice system of exchange.

Cash, the Black Lab

Another story my pet mom told me about had to do with a friend of hers who had heart trouble and was alone in her house when she became ill. This woman was having a heart attack when her black lab realized something was terribly wrong. He licked her face to keep her awake and then tugged on her shirtsleeve, dragging her across two halls and the kitchen floor to where the telephone was. He brought the cradle of the phone down to her level on the floor and pushed the emergency button on the phone for her, thus saving her life.

Trifles and Truffles

Trifles and Truffles, two very brave black cats, saved the house of another woman my pet mom knows when their old electric blanket caught on fire. The cats screeched and scratched under the closed door of the bedroom where their pet sitter was sleeping until they were able to wake her up. Because of Trifles and Truffles alerting their pet sitter quickly, the firefighters were able to come and put out the fire before there was too much damage done. The owner of the house was able to beautify her old house with new rugs and wallpaper because her cats intervened in time. These cats are heroes!

Karla's Celestial Thoughts

Healing with Nature

I talk to rocks, I talk to trees,
They all have such good energy.
Nature shows us how to heal,
In ways mysterious, yet real.

Leaning on a willow tree,
I'm suddenly at peace.
Feeling life is wonderful,
I find a great release.

Once, walking by a river bank,
A rock gleamed in bright sunlight.
This rock was made of crystal,
And a sparkling, shiny sight.

I just had to bring this rock back home,
Although it was quite heavy.
We pushed it up a hill together;
Joe was very steady.

Rocks bring healing, and centering,
Helping a person to cope.
They show one courage and fortitude,
Always bringing hope.

In northern California, there was
A rock we had to keep,
Although sending it to Minnesota
Was a very tricky feat.

Sometimes one simply can't explain,
Why one must have a certain rock,
Or why it calls out to you -
But you clearly hear it talk.

There were pine cones in the
Carolinas,
I brought some of them home.
Also, shells from Florida,
With their own healing tones.

When nature starts to talk to you,
You never are the same again.
Even when you can't explain it,
Nature is your friend.

Karla and the Crystal Rock

*Our kids
rock climbing*

Heart to Heart Talks

Before Pierre arrived at our house, we had a mixed breed dog - part Collie, part Labrador and also part Coyote. Casper lived in a pen outside but was let out every day to play and to interact with the family. Casper was a very friendly white dog with a huge smile permanently highlighting his face. He would curl his lips up and grin at anyone or anything that came his way.

When Snagglepuss the outdoor cat first arrived at the house, Joe introduced him to Casper. He explained to Casper that he must be friends with Snagglepuss and that he shouldn't chase him but should treat him respectfully.

"Snagglepuss is part of the family now," Joe told him. He knew that Casper tended to chase anything in his path, especially rabbits in the area.

As Joe talked to him, Casper perked up his ears and listened carefully. When Joe let him out of his pen a few minutes later, he bounded out as usual, raced around the yard in circles as he often did and then ran full speed over to Snagglepuss.

Casper, the friendly dog

I held my breath as I watched this drama unfold but Casper stopped on a dime when he reached Snagglepuss and just stood there in front of him, nose to nose. Snagglepuss, who had also been listening to Joe's talk, did not hiss as he tended to do with any other creature. Thus, a great friendship between the two of them took hold. Animals understand our needs and what we want from them; we just have to give them a chance.

On Telling the Truth

I have a friend who is a pet mom to two miniature schnauzers. This lady travels a lot, but just before she leaves for the airport she has these two dogs sit down in front of her by the door while she explains to them where she is going, how long she will be gone and when she will be back. They perk up their ears and listen to every word, behaving very well with their pet sitters while their pet mom is gone, knowing she will be back soon. Animals want the truth so we humans should be honest with them because they understand everything we say.

The Coon Condo

I had the unusual opportunity to visit friends who were raising nine raccoons. It was summer and the coons were already three months old, living happily in a wooden framed structure with screen windows on all sides. When I got there, the raccoons rushed out of their wooden shelter, curious to see who was visiting them. They seemed to be socialized and unafraid, which made interacting with them fun and easy. When we stepped inside the 'raccoon condo,' I noticed a wading pool formed in the dirt floor where my friends had supplied their furry friends with some minnows. No wonder they liked their home so much! I sat on the floor with my new furry friends, laughing as they crawled onto my feet and attempted to untie the laces of my shoes. I admired their dark, sharp eyes peering at me from inside their bandit masks. One of them crawled up my body to investigate my necklace, handling it with extremely dexterous paws while the close inspection was underway.

Seeing these raccoons up close was an extremely rewarding experience. Like all animals, they communicate in their own way, exerting their unique intuitive abilities to their surroundings. I am grateful for people like these friends of mine who have saved dozens of raccoons, caring for them until they can be slowly reintroduced to the wild.

Jamaica on Earth Day

My first grand dog -
we didn't get to say good-bye,
which makes me want to sigh,
And yet I wish to say, I do believe she knows -
This Black and Tan coon dog with a giant soul.

She used to love to mountain climb and carried her own backpack,
Jamaica was courageous - this is just a fact.
She calmly loved humans, almost everyone she met,
And had a serene countenance, I never will forget.

They buried her atop a mountain,
and planted a cherry tree on her grave -
This dog with inner calm and loving nature -
Jamaica, oh so swift and brave.
And her shining spirit forever continues to thrive,
As she climbs the mountains in the sky.

Look on the Bright Side

Through the years I have learned a great deal about healing. I have come to understand how important it is to keep a positive attitude and to see the bright side of things, even when dealing with an illness. I believe we are sometimes put through tests because we have life lessons to work through. It's good to laugh a lot; it makes you feel lighter, which can make it easier to heal. That's one of the reasons why it is good to have pets – they can be very healing for humans to be around. Animals help us to laugh and play. They also help us to create by bringing out our lighter side. We are distracted from our worries and concerns as we shift our focus to taking care of them and to enjoying their companionship. They give us a purpose in life and many of the antics pets do will lighten our hearts if we are having a bad day.

Sometimes a flower or plant can be healing, too. Just like pets, they bring happiness into our lives just by being around. It can be very healing to go out and dig in the garden. Growing things can bring you joy and make you feel much better. To see an awesome sunrise or spectacular sunset is yet another way to experience healing. The oceans, the forests, the mountains, the winding river - there are so many healing attributes to nature.

Animals can show us courage and bravery, and they are very protective. We can learn from the animals about how to be strong and how to face the world with faith. Pets are unselfish and give such unconditional love that they will sometimes put themselves in danger to help their pet family.

Animals lower the blood pressure of humans, bring joy and laughter into our lives and show us how to live courageously. We need to help and rescue them whenever they need it. We need to be there for them, too. We should talk honestly to them and of course, always treat them with kindness.

6
Visiting with a Fairy

Pierre's Philosophy

I dreamt one night that I spoke with a fairy. Her name was Fairy Lily and she was absolutely beautiful. She had pink and purple wings that were bigger than she was. She also had beautiful yellow colored hair, blue eyes and a radiant smile. I traveled to her land of little people and saw amazing sights.

There were fairies working together, and elves and gnomes trying to bring healing and love to this earth. They were all out in a swamp near the woods. It was summer and the fairies were intermingling with the lightning bugs so it was hard to distinguish them from one another.

Fairy Lily sat on top of a huge lily pad in the lake near shore. The lake was bluish, shining and luminous as the full moon beamed down upon it. Fairies are very elusive and it is difficult to ever find one who will stay still long enough to talk because they like to stay in motion, or in hiding, and can be rather shy with others. However, an astral traveling cat can slip in just about anywhere.

It was a wonderful July night when all of the earth was aglow with magic. It was humid and warm. Crickets were chirping, frogs were croaking and creatures from other dimensions seemed to be converging in a giant, pulsating, wonderfully positive energy.

Fairy Lily had a lilting voice that reminded me of a cooing bird. She decided to talk to me for a while. I felt honored as I sat on shore,

gazing at her. She told me many things that night and passed on much
of her wisdom, wishing to share it with me.

A Gift from the Lake

In a sad voice, Fairy Lily said that we must save the environment.
Humans have been so busy destroying the environment that there
are fewer fairies, elves and gnomes than there used to be. Hopefully
humankind is beginning to awaken and will be able to save the world
before it is too late.

These are challenging times. There is still magic in the world
but we must realize Mother Earth needs to be treated with love and
respect. She has loved us and has been very good to us. We should
remember to love and be good to her in return.

Fairy Lily then said she must leave. In a whirlwind of mystical
beauty, she fluttered her wings and ascended to the skies. I sighed and
flipped back into my body, falling back to sleep again at the household,
filled with appreciation for this marvelous journey.

Karla's Celestial Thoughts

When I was a very little girl, my older sister and brother both
claimed one night that they saw a fairy come flying through our upstairs
bedroom window to visit us. I was delighted but surprised to hear such
a thing and they always repeated the same story whenever I asked
them. I believe them now. Many magical things happen that people
cannot explain. Children are often more tuned in to other worlds than
adults are. Sometimes children remember past lives, as they have not
been told yet that this is not acceptable.

A Wood Elf

I was fortunate to have a magical experience with my son and
husband years later. I believe the "little people" really exist because of
this strange experience the three of us shared. Our family was driving
home from our cabin in northern Minnesota and our youngest son was

sitting in the front seat with my husband and me. There were woods on both sides of the road and it was nearing dusk. This part of the trip is in very wild country where there are very few cars around.

Suddenly, the three of us in the front seat witnessed something astonishing - a tiny little man wearing a green outfit with a green pointed hat, and carrying a pail. He jumped up from the ditch in the road in front of us and scurried across the road, about twenty feet away. All three of us witnessed the same thing. This little man rushed from one side of this old dirt road to the other and disappeared into the woods. Our youngest son said, "Well, there goes an elf." It was a wondrous experience, which I will never forget!

The Fairy Ring

One day I decided to create a fairy ring in our little woods in which to meditate. As I sat inside the circle I asked the fairies to show me they were really around and to give me physical evidence that they truly were communicating with me. I was uncertain how this evidence would come but felt something would happen. Three days later I was walking in these same woods and noticed something new. Almost overnight, it would seem, there were huge white mushroom puffballs growing. We had never seen these mushroom puffballs before, ever! The first year I counted ten of them. The second year there

Karla and the Magic Puffballs

were fourteen. The appearance of these unusual mushrooms was very
mysterious.

Nature Teaches Us Love

Aquariums with slow moving fish can be mesmerizing.
With soothing waters so relaxing, they can be hypnotizing.
Parakeets with cheery songs may awaken one each day,
Singing through their repertoire in a chirping bright display.

Hamsters peddling on their wheels, these fuzzy little creatures,
With busyness and active lives their most endearing features.
A frog in a terrarium, croaking late at night.
She hops and peeks around the plants, a fascinating sight.

The loyal dog who loves you, as so many cats do, too.
They all enrich our lives so much, in the many things they do
Pets make us laugh and bring us joy - extensions of ourselves.
They light up all of our lives so much, as in our hearts they dwell.

Or sometimes when you venture out, you may find the trees will talk.
As you commune with nature while out going for a walk.
Do they ever seem to murmur, or to pat you, or to sigh,
As you are sauntering along, or simply walking by?

There was a tree our daughter used to talk to every day.
It grew up extra strong, and like her, also made its way.
Bushes and flowers, rocks and trees, they all have such good energy.
Nature is so beautiful if we will only stop and see.

Animals enrich our lives and seem to make us more aware,
The simple things in life are very joyful, if we will but care.
From the stars in this huge universe to the starfish of the sea,
We learn of love and healing in life's glorious mystery.

Mother Earth, Our Big Mom

Has anyone ever studied
How the world became so muddied,
Abused badly and most bloodied,
Yet, I think she has great soul.

This is our gem, dear Mother Earth,
A diamond of tremendous worth,
And to save her should be our unending goal.

Some people cannot breathe in cities,
The situation is not pretty,
There is acid rain now pouring down,
And less pure water still around.

We have contaminated seas,
We still are cutting many trees,
With our own selfish and exaggerated needs.

To show our Mother that we care,
To recognize, we each must dare.
And even with pollution,
There still are some solutions.

But it depends on our help and attitude,
And that is not just a platitude.
We really need to pick up trash,
And in the right way have it stashed.

Recycle clothes, give to the poor,
And please I really do implore,
Go plant a tree, or a new seed,
As renewal also is the key.
We have not shown our Mother that we cared in our past history.

We are one speck in this universe,
Still our attitudes must be reversed.
Mother Earth needs help and respect,
Something we should not forget.
Next time you see a can along the side of some old road,
Pick it up, dispose of it, and help Earth's giant load.

Mother Nature cannot mend,
If we ignore her and just pretend.
We must awaken to her needs,
And show affection for her indeed,
In order that we may all succeed.

She raised us, and it's payback time, as we must show her we care.
To mend, to heal, to save her soul, we must be more aware.
We pollute the air, the water, the earth,
and must be made to understand,
We must attempt some sort of plan to save this world,
our precious land!

Elf Land Experience

While on a trip to Bayfield, Wisconsin one year, I talked to the owner of a little store who told me the wee little people were sometimes found on Madeline Island, down by a lagoon. A friend and I were going over to the island, but at this point I had never been there before and got very excited to meet someone who also believed in elves and fairies. My friend and I had gone our separate ways for an hour and then were going to meet each other and decide where to go next.

Whenever I pray for validation I get it, sometimes almost immediately. The very next store I went to was an art store where I met a woman who had just started working there. She had a magical vibration to her and I knew I should talk to her. We started chatting about an elf picture that was in her store and out of the blue she told me she had seen elves over on the island. For some reason, she said, she felt I would understand if she told me this. Two people in the same day saying the same thing, and not the usual thing! We did go to the lagoon and I felt elf energies all around. I know they were there working their magic. I immediately found a flat grey rock about four inches in diameter, which had a beautiful scene of an ocean wave on top of it. It is one of my treasures from the water and I have it to this day.

The Real Fairy

There is a small, bright lady whom I think could be a fairy.
She has pure fairy energies which she always carries.
In this world she has had troubles as it can be hard to live on earth.
She is extremely sensitive, and has been since her birth.

Why should people judge if people have a different way,
How can people really know - how can people say.
There are so many things in life which cannot be explained,
Many ways in this wide world which might seem very strange.

I know this person tries so hard - she is a shining light.
Sometimes she has lost her way, but yet tries to do right.
I believe that she is now okay, and learning on her own,
I am so very proud of her - how she has truly grown.

7
Meandering with Monica
Facing Fears

Pierre's Philosophy

A few years ago, one of my pet mom's relatives went to Arizona for the winter and asked my pet mom to spider-sit her tarantula. She thought the road trip and the desert heat would be too much for Monica the tarantula, so my pet mom agreed to take care of her for the winter. At the time the arrangement was thought to be a temporary one, but perhaps not surprisingly, Monica is still with us all these years later. As I have said before, pets choose which humans they want to be with!

Even though she was a bit intimidated by Monica, my pet mom was willing to give her a chance and to try and get to know her better. She went to great lengths to create an environment for Monica that would not cause any disturbance for me, believing I would also be intimidated by the spider's presence. I did notice Monica's terrarium on top of the small, free standing cabinet just outside the kitchen. I was a bit curious about this new black fuzzy creature but not curious enough to risk jumping up on the terrarium where there was no room to maneuver. I knew the glass cage and I would probably both go flying across the room. Sometimes it is best to let a sleeping dog lie, or a sleeping tarantula as the case may be.

I realized my pet mom needed this experience so she could learn that strange, scary creatures can be good, too. I saw my pet mom go through quite a transformation as the winter weeks went on. She faithfully brought home six live crickets for Monica each week. She also did some research about how to take care of tarantulas, so she would be more aware of Monica's needs.

Strangers Bearing Gifts

My pet mom told me about a frightening dream she had when Monica first came to live in our home. She dreamed Monica and I had met and could not figure out what to make of each other. However, after that first night my pet mom did not have any more fearful dreams about Monica.

As time went on, my pet mom started to wonder about the messages exotic creatures have to bring to the world. No sooner had she started wondering about this when she ran into a snake and then the next day, a salamander on her daily walk. She had not seen unusual creatures like this in years but now they were just appearing in her path as if eager to encourage her train of thought. Both creatures made her more aware of the beauty of the creepy crawlies and made her realize they have a place in life too, even though one might not think they are that appealing. My pet mom was surprised to see these two creatures so soon after wondering about them but when you pray for answers, they do arrive.

Give everyone a chance. Be discerning and aware, and yet willing to learn and give other creatures, human or otherwise, a chance in life. Be brave. Even things that scare you can bring gifts and lessons.

Monica meandering around

Karla's Celestial Thoughts

Facing the Monster

I used to have a disturbing dream in which a monster kept chasing me and scaring me at night, almost every night for a week. This upsetting dream made me very uneasy. One day I decided this was ridiculous and that if I dreamt it again I was going to face up to my fear. That night when again I encountered this horrible, hairy black monster chasing me down a narrow alley, I turned around and it literally bumped into me. It felt very slimy and although I felt like recoiling in fear, I stood there and screamed at it instead.

"You are not real, and there is no way you can hurt me! I am not afraid of you!"

I watched as the monster began to fade and melt before my very eyes and then I realized it was just a hologram, a surreal vision, not even real. It disappeared and I never had that dream again.

House of Horror

Years ago when my son Eric was away at art school, he was staying temporarily at a rooming house that I felt had a bad aura to it - bad vibrations. Once when I was visiting him, we went to the music room downstairs and I noticed that the feeling down in the basement was especially creepy.

I kept visualizing a white light around him and his roommates during the time he stayed at this old house because the sense I had of the place made me nervous. In the intuitive world, visualizing a white light of protection around someone can create a buffer zone of safety. It is like putting out a shielding energy field.

During one visit, I slept overnight in his room while Eric slept on a couch in the living room. I played Elvis gospel music on the stereo, and by mistake I hit the wrong button so it kept replaying all night. I think this actually increased the good vibrations in his room and in the house.

The house was robbed a week later and although the thief got away, he dropped a gun by the hall window on his way out. My son's room was the only room not ransacked. The night I helped my son move out, my guide, Keeno, told me to be a "spiritual warrior." I was nervous about leaving the place and glad when we put the last load in our car.

Some time after that, we found out that years before Eric had moved into that house, people used to shoot heroin in the basement. No wonder I had sensed bad entities around!

Some buildings have bad vibrations. I have learned much over the years about how to clear these bad energies, using sage, prayers and spiritual ceremonies. Often, one can encourage negative energy to move on. On this occasion however, I was just happy to get Eric out of that place. We left a positive healing rock in the basement when my son moved out but it would have taken so much more to get good energy back into the house. We needed to get out.

Phantom Dog

One winter night I walked outside to feed our two dogs and came upon a huge and extremely menacing black dog sitting between the two pens, staring at me and growling. The dogs in their pens did not seem to notice him, which was really odd. I did not dare get close to this dog, and because of the way in which he was positioned between the two pens and the doors, I could not get to the entrances of the two pens to feed our own dogs.

This phantom dog was growling and looked like it wanted to move towards me and attack. I felt he could be rabid. He did not have a collar on him and had eerie looking reddish eyes. Finally my son came home but when I showed him the dog by shining a flashlight on him from a distance across the yard, he did not know what to do either.

I decided real or not, this dog was testing me. So armed with a large pan and spoon, I got in our car, turned on the motor and drove the vehicle close to him, making a lot of commotion by speeding up to him and stopping sharply. Opening the car door and racing at him, I pounded the pan loudly with the spoon and yelled forcefully, "Noooooo!" As I went roaring up to him, he stood as still as stone for a most intense moment and then turned and took off across the lake on the ice with his tail between his legs. I conquered my fear as I faced him, and he was gone. He never came back again.

It seems to me that bad spirits sometimes test us.

Negativity

I know there are negative forces in the world, but we should not give them power by playing into them with fear. Instead, we should fight them with healing and light, sending good energy to break up the bad. Even though I faced the phantom dog, I also sent him good vibrations after he left.

Dark things in life only have power over you if you give in to fear. You conquer negativity with courage and good thoughts. There is much suffering and pain in the world, it's true, but I believe a person can keep his or her balance in difficult situations by requesting the guidance of angels and the light of protection, and by calling on and believing in the power of God.

To cleanse an area and to bring good energies into a place, use a smudge stick to release the negative energy wherever you need it, or use incense and say prayers. Another method to use for cleansing is drumming, which breaks up negative energy and creates a higher vibration of good. Also, picturing a white light around yourself or others you are concerned about is very protective and truly works.

Monica's Message

I baby-sat a South American spider,
now why on earth would I invite her?
Sometimes if judgment makes us blind,
we should leave prejudice behind.
This tarantula I baby-sat is quite a charming acrobat.
She creeps and crawls her way around,
head in the clouds, feet on the ground.

She seems outrageous, I admit, and yet my view changed bit by bit.
If we give nature half a chance, no matter what our circumstance,
We learn life's lessons as we grow - to reach past fear expands the soul.
Too often people live in fear, refuse to see, refuse to hear.

Because of her, I asked to be shown the beauty of the deep unknown.
A message came back right away, on my nature walk the very next day.
I had not seen a snake in years, and by my path one slithered near.
Two days later I walked again,
and discovered another of nature's friends.

A salamander, bright orange and brown,
slowly sauntered across the ground.
I walked that same path many days,
and these creatures never came my way.
But this I truly do believe - if you ask for a message you will receive.
Now, I am not afraid to try new things, and find beauty in everything.

All of God's creatures have their place,
although some we don't know, or cannot face.
So Monica stayed here for a while,
and there are reasons why I smile.
As I was given an interesting option;
she could be mine through an adoption.
In this giant world she did her part -
this one lone spider touched my heart.

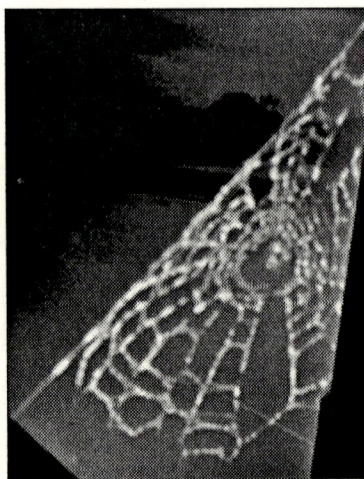

Spider Lace

8
Predator or Friend – Being Discerning

Pierre's Philosophy

It can be challenging to discern who is a friend and who is a foe. Sometimes I am a naive pussycat, I admit it. I trust most people and creatures and yet can usually figure out a bad apple in the bunch, as the humans would say.

Once I had a dream in which I was in the little woods that I can see from our bay window. There was a seemingly innocent brown owl that swept down onto a high branch and stared at me with piercing, golden eyes. This creature tried to entice me into coming closer to it, and with those hypnotic eyes he tried to lure me with the promise of telling me some of nature's secrets. Well, I was not born yesterday and I backed away, telling this fierce creature that I did not think it was a good idea. His pasty smile turned into a scowl as he flew off into the black night to find other prey. Even though this was a dream, I shuddered at what he really wanted to teach me - no doubt what a good lunch I would be for him!

What I have learned is that there are charmers in the world. It is essential that we use our awareness to identify the true intentions of those we encounter. Give people a chance, yet be aware of predators.

The Visitors

My pet mom once baby-sat a child who was very noisy, and there have also been other guests in our household who were very loud. I have to hide under beds. I wait until they leave and then I come out again. I like peace and quiet. I just want to love people and to be loved back. What else is there in the world?

Sometimes I get my back up and feel threatened, but I really don't like to be on the defensive. If this does become necessary though, I simply puff myself up to look bigger. It seems to make people realize they should not mess with me. If you don't show fear, bullies will often back off. Sometimes one has to take a stand, even if the offense is unintentional. Once when a visitor at our home stepped on my tail by mistake, I tried to quietly pull it out from under her. When that did not work, I meowed loudly to get her attention. I don't like to complain but sometimes these tall people, the humans, are just not aware.

Sometimes visitors can really be cat lovers but they don't realize they are too loud or too excitable. You should approach an animal slowly, or wait for us to approach you. We know which humans are cat lovers but it may take a while to earn our trust.

Karla's Celestial Thoughts

We were on the back streets of Paris, my friend and I, trying to hail a cab to leave a bad area of town we had inadvertently walked into. I was carrying some pink variegated yarn I was going to make into an afghan for my friend when we got back to America. The street became more and more seedy, until finally we both silently prayed, and almost immediately a cab appeared from out of nowhere. We were able to hurry out of this negative area and on to safer streets.

I love Paris - it is a very exciting, stimulating, exhilarating city, but this day had been difficult. We ended up at the wrong place, and in the wrong area of town. I felt like there were predators all around us. When we eventually got back to America, I did make an afghan and presented it to my friend who, I think, doubly appreciated it knowing what we had gone through to get that yarn.

A predator can be a supposed friend who is only interested in using you. I think everyone has had a few of them in his or her life, or perhaps even a relative who is very difficult. Still, one should not regret being a caring, loving person. One should not feel foolish for making the mistake of sometimes trusting the wrong people. Just pick up your life and move on. Take the high road. Don't hate, but let go. Sometimes we cannot love or forgive another person for some injustice, but we can let go and separate ourselves from their energy.

Eiffel Tower of Paris

One of the ways to do this is to sit alone and think about all of the reasons you are mad at the person and then write them down. When you are satisfied you have expressed your feelings on paper, say,

"I release you from my life and no longer feel tied to you. I may not love you or even be able to forgive you but I do let you go. I am separate from your energy."

I have had clients who told me this works well for them. If you write about a painful experience you want to put behind you, burning the pages in a ceremony can work wonders. Letting go is very healing.

Cutting the Cord

Though the energies that bind us to others may not be visible, they are as real as any ropes or chains we can see with our eyes. Another way to release someone from one's life is to perform a ceremony I call "Cutting the Cord."

Place two chairs facing each other at a comfortable distance apart. Tie one end of the yarn, string or rope to one of the chairs and then sitting in the opposite chair, tie the other end around your waist.

Imagine the person you would like to separate from is sitting in the chair in front of you. Go through all of the thoughts and feelings you have about this person, vocalizing the injustices he or she has committed. Don't hold back. When you feel you have finished, cut the rope with a scissors, saying, "I release you and am no longer affected by you. You are not in my life. I wish you well in the future."

While we strive to nurture and care for others, we must be mindful that there are users in the world. Learning discernment is an important part of honoring yourself and safeguarding your vital energy.

Beyond the Rainbow

I dreamed about a rainbow in the sky.
This waltzing, dancing ribbon caught my eye.
This streamer shone with clarity and I understood.
Always there is hope in life, so recognize the good.
You may have a friend or relative with whom you can't see eye to eye.
And there may be a rift you can't deny.

Someday, beyond the rainbow, you both may understand,
Far, far away, and in another land.
Perennial friends are here for us in any kind of weather.
They love us unconditionally in all of our endeavors.
Still, sometimes in a friendship there are obstacles you feel,
Sometimes insurmountable, with which you have to deal.

A priest advised me long ago, some problems can't be solved.
Some relationships or situations cannot be resolved.
But this rainbow, like a moving prism shining in the sky,
Gives me faith and courage, and still makes me want to try.
If we listen to ourselves, and we stay true to our beliefs,
We stand by our convictions and we find abiding peace.

If we remain quite centered - to adversity we won't react.
Our souls are bathed in truthfulness, our energy intact.
Some friends we lose, some friends we gain.
Perennial friends will still remain.
Friendships based on honesty are forever nourished.
If they are based on faith and love, they will forever flourish.

Now, I am most determined to always do my best.
And with a positive attitude, my life is very blessed.
Someday beyond the rainbow, these same people we may meet,
As we reunite with joyful understanding, not defeat.
So thank heaven for all friendships and the lessons we may learn.
Even if most difficult, there are blessings in return.

Thank heaven for our relatives, however hard some might be.
There still are lessons here for us, in our personal history.
Thank heaven for my rainbow dream - God's hope for you and me.
When things can't be resolved, stay centered, with pure energy.
Nature teaches lessons if we listen to her melody.
Spirit has the answer - that we still can live in harmony.

Another night I had a dream where this rainbow was shattered,
And even though it burst forth with combustion - still what mattered?
As conflict brought new understanding, and lives were rearranged.
Sometimes true enlightenment comes, as our lives are changed.
So never, ever give up hope - you never know where things will lead,
And sometimes in the darkest hour, you find you will succeed.

9
Thor Streaker:
Weathering the Storms of Life

Pierre's Philosophy

I have been the most pampered, petted, stroked, combed, brushed, and spoiled creature in this household for 19 years. My pet mom never had another indoor pet so that I wouldn't have to go through the stress of adjusting. I have had her all to myself. I think she knew I was her familiar, her other half, and her helper throughout the last two decades.

Other creatures did enter the picture, however, rounding out the lives of the family, who apparently needed a bit of diversity to learn different lessons. I could have told them Streak was going to be a real test for them but they needed to find it out for themselves. He was a challenge from the beginning. However, pets do choose you and I think he was here to teach my pet mom many things, one of which was patience and how to cope with different situations and problems.

My pet mom would have me sit on her lap while she told me the ongoing story of Streak. He was a dysfunctional dog who arrived on their doorstep one day - filthy, starving, and with many burrs in his long brown, black and white fur. Streak eventually became friends with Casper, who by then was old and had a tumor on his side. Streak was very protective of him. He would round him up and help him

if any other dogs came around, even though Casper was perfectly
capable of taking care of himself. They became good friends, although
it took a while.

Streak was incredibly high strung. If somebody raised a hand the
slightest bit, he would cringe. When he heard loud noises, like lightning
or a gunshot or fireworks, he would run away. My feline intuition told
me he had been abused and left in the wild to fend for himself. He had
a hard time bonding with anyone, preferring to spend his time hunting
in the brush. His favorite pastime was sniffing for rabbits or some
other creature with his nose close to the ground, like Sherlock Holmes.
Streak never obeyed anyone when he was hunting, and when he wasn't
hunting, which was rare, he did not do much better. He had his own
program, whatever it was.

Once, after hours and hours of Streak playing in the marsh and
running back and forth, my pet mom became frustrated so she decided
to stand in a strategic spot in the swamp in order to catch him. Wearing
high boots, she literally tackled Streak as he trotted by her. She put
a leash on him so she could bring him back to feed him in his pen.
Otherwise he would hunt forever, as only a stubborn Springer Spaniel
can do, and with enough energy for ten dogs in just his wiggling
hindquarters and tail alone.

It was very difficult for Streak to trust anyone and that was the
lesson of this dog - to love him anyway. He had been so abused,
and could not connect with anyone very well. Sometimes there are
creatures out there that have a hard time connecting or bonding with
humans. Try to see and appreciate their value anyway, as they have
their place in the world, too. Abuse takes such a toll on any creature,
animal or human, and should not be tolerated. People need to become
more aware so they can stop abuse. We animals have feelings, so don't
think we are unaware. We have hearts and souls, too. Every human,
animal, plant, tree, bird, or fish is connected to each other somehow,
so whatever is done to one of us affects all others. We are all in this
together.

Streaker with a lopsided halo

Karla's Celestial Thoughts

I believe we all have our own family constellations agreed upon before we are born, and waiting to come into this world. Fortunately, my family was basically happy with a lot of love to share and give. We also had some shadows – the darkest of which was alcoholism. One can be a victim or a survivor in life and I chose to be a survivor. The trouble with drinking is that it can be abusive and hard on your soul. Those living with or around an addicted person may be neglected instead of nurtured and it can be difficult to get through.

What I learned from living with alcoholism was to depend on spirituality and look to God and the angels for help. This is what got me through some tough times. I asked God for help and received answers. As I grew up, I learned to love myself. I was an odd fit for my family and felt like I was not understood when I was younger. However, as I grew older I was able to find people who understood and even helped me appreciate my gifts. Over time my family has come to appreciate my unusual nature, too.

Facing Addiction

So many people are in denial about addictions or abuse in their families. There is a ripple effect across the entire family that goes unnoticed when people are in denial. Being validated for your feelings can be very important, and finding people who understand you creates the support you need to move forward. Being honest, even though it is painful, is the healthiest way. I realize I don't have to be a caretaker to the world unless I want to be. I learned to say no to people and feel okay with it, and to talk about my feelings. I am now able to honor and take care of myself first.

Although it took me a while, I eventually learned to find my voice and speak my truth. When you have alcoholism in the family you learn to be a caretaker and internalize your feelings, which can make life difficult. This caretaker behavior often becomes so automatic, one is not even aware of it. Life does get better, though, as one's awareness increases and understanding grows. I found it is important to not be a victim but to use the experience as a tool for growth instead. We all have wounds to deal with in life. I now prefer to focus on the good things in our family, of which there are many! My parents are both gone now but in my heart I thank them for the many marvelous gifts they have helped shape in me: an appreciation of life, a sense of humor, an education and a love for helping the world.

Joe and I were honest with our children when they were growing up, talking to them about the alcoholism in my family. I wanted them to know the situation. We had some dear friends who went through treatment for drinking, and we took our kids (who were then pre-adolescents) to the treatment center while we visited them. It was visitor's day so there were quite a few people there. It was good for our kids to see that these were just regular people from all walks of life who were brave enough to seek help. One of the great lessons of that place was in feeling the spirit of the people, to know they were receiving help, and to see how important it is to have families, friends and faith.

East Meets West

East meets West,
Both paths are blessed,
With prayer or meditation, either way you go.
Many ways have meaning, many ways have soul.

Turbulent Storms of Life

People can be lonely, overwhelmed, or feeling sad.
Sometimes they have deep, dark pain, or a situation very bad.
In spite of any difficulties, they may find a way.
It is so true, I have always found, things happen when you pray.

All of life is meaningful - God hears every sigh.
He recognizes every soul and knows whenever we try.
If it seems quite hopeless with one's life in complete shambles,
Shake the feeling, get a grip, and take action as you scramble.

If you have a little faith and take a chance on God,
Even though life's storms are huge, He is a lightning rod.
With life's swirling tornadoes, you still have a safety zone.
Even in great turbulence, you are not alone.

Let the light come in, and open windows of your heart.
Recognize the world does need you - you have your own part.
Do not be discouraged; as life changes you evolve.
Be brave and have some courage, and your problems will dissolve.

The earth has its own melodies; be quiet, listen to the sounds.
With faith and a good attitude, you may turn your life around.
There is somebody up there, though we may be unaware.
I've always known within my heart, there is a God who cares.

As the storms then dissipate, angels bring a sun so bright.
Bluebirds sing sweet rhapsodies and suddenly the world has light.
Now, I believe in angels, and I call upon them every day.
Every time I ask them, they will clearly show the way.

God is Color Blind

If a person is white, black, yellow, red, brown, or even green,
A space alien unseen,
They should not be judged.
If they are gay or straight, bisexual, or asexual,
Fat or thin, plain or beautiful,
Simple or smart, dull or brilliant,
They should not be judged.

If they have short hair or long, or no hair,
If they are poor or rich, a farmer, a butcher,
a lawyer, a waitress, a doctor,
Or if they are withdrawn or outgoing, flighty or methodical,
Emotional or logical, ignorant or educated, atheists or religious,
They still should not be judged.

If they are a woman or man, young or old,
Sick or well, weak or strong, right handed or left,
They should not be judged.

The important things should be
Kindness, respect, fairness, honesty, and integrity.
And the bottom line should be LOVE.
And how do we know unless we are in another person's shoes,
What life has brought him or her, or why they are the way they are.

Leave prejudice behind,
And be like God - color blind.

Plowing up the Garden

Pain so serious, suffering so bad,
a heart feels delirious, broken and sad.
How can those days of loving ever be erased,
times of deep happiness cannot be replaced.
Love can be flowing, growing, always in life's garden.
It blossoms or it grows, or it unfortunately may harden.

This heart needed healing, yet I knew it would mend.
Even though it was not easy, and in fact hard to pretend.
And still, this person found, that two years down the line,
New love entered her life again, and she was feeling fine.

Petty Tyrants

You may happen across petty tyrants in this world, but you should not let them bother you. Keep centered so you can grow. People who are manipulative or controlling need to be handled with care. If you do not buy into their foolishness and ignorance you will be fine. If they attempt to drag you down, you have a choice and sometimes need to talk back, but other times need to simply ignore them. Controlling people are frustrated when they cannot get to you, and will eventually direct their focus elsewhere. Unfortunately, there are negative people in the world who are difficult but it is a true triumph to overcome, to override and to transcend.

Music in their Souls

We listen with our hearts to hear the music in their souls.
These special people in the world enrich our lives more than they know.
Blessed are the handicapped, whom we should never forget.
Though vulnerable to the whole world, they are deserving of respect.

I worked once at a group home for adults who were quite handicapped.
It is amazing how in life they manage to adapt.
Courageously they cope with things, much more than they may show.
They bravely face more obstacles than we could ever know.

Yet always there is hope for things that they try to achieve.
You have to have a faith in them, you really must believe.
The residents will sometimes fight, yet quickly they forgive.
Such lessons we can learn as they teach others how to live.

They have a sense of humor that is wonderful to feel.
Their love of life is genuine, and all of their feelings real.
With them one can have patience and find joy in little things.
They see life with such honesty in what is happening.

Now, listen and you too may hear the music of their souls.
When tuned into the positive, we find we all can grow.
It really is that simple too, when all is said and done.
The melody they teach is love - they touch the lives of everyone.

The Jail Sentence

Sometimes people make mistakes, do wrong, and go to jail.
These people are quite fearful, and their whole lives are derailed.
If they find a faith and pray, answers truly come.
They may find faith in themselves, even if they are the only one.

With rehabilitation, which is necessary too,
Criminals do pay the price - they have to pay their dues.
Yes, people make mistakes, it does not mean they will again,
And if they trust in God, they may find Spirit is their friend.

Silent Tears

For the baby who was lost,
At what a terrible cost,
Whether by miscarriage or by abortion,
It is difficult to keep the loss in proportion.

I know a woman who always counts her children as five,
Even though she has just three of them alive.
These souls are not forgotten, and they have a part,
As these special souls can still live within one's heart.

This soul can be an angel on the other side,
Or this soul can be still with the woman as a guide.
Nothing is ever truly lost,
Although it may be at quite a cost.

Or a soul may come through again, another time, another place.
That soul may be recycled again, to come another day.
No one should judge abortion,
nor can one know what another goes through.
Only God knows the reasons for what a person has to do.

Holocaust, Hellish Hurricane

I met a woman who lived through the holocaust,
Where she lost all of her family and friends.
She will never really be all right, but she did survive.
Amazingly, she still believes, although she grieves,
That she must forgive, so she can live,
This wise old soul.

And although she said she has nightmares,
Remembering her loved ones every day helps.
And though some of the horrors she cannot forget,
She becomes quite balanced, as she still believes in God's love,
And still has faith in angels up above.

The Purple Heart

Years ago, I was out at the lake visiting my mother's neighbor,
Roy, an old bachelor who was also a World War II veteran. While my
kids sat on my mother's front porch, he had come over to see us but
did not seem like his usual cheerful self. He generally loved teasing
and playing with my kids. However, on this day he seemed very sad.

My kids were running around, not paying any attention to us, so
I decided it was a good time to ask him what was wrong. He looked
startled but got tears in his eyes and said he was having bad dreams
again. Apparently, he had been having nightmares ever since the war
and every now and again they would bother him so much he couldn't
sleep. He talked of having to kill people and feeling guilty about it,
and about seeing good friends in his unit die. He sat there on this
beautiful sunny autumn day with deep pain in his eyes, talking about
the war. He said he would be okay but that his dreams disturbed him
sometimes.

I was a young mother, thinking about what to give my kids for dinner that night and about how they would be dirty and would need baths. I imagined my life to be so busy and full; how could I even begin to understand what Roy was going through? Nevertheless, I tried. When Roy asked if I wanted to see his Purple Heart, I signaled my mother to keep the kids outside and followed him into his house. Roy proudly produced the cherished medal, and I admired it, thinking about how easily we take our freedom for granted. It seems we seldom stop to realize how much has been given to us in America, or how blessed we are. And so, I held Roy's Purple Heart as he blew his nose and we both cried. Then, we walked back out into the sunshine where the laughter of my children seemed to bring him back to his usual cheery mood.

I will always thank heaven for the Roys of the world.

Changing, Rearranging

Sometimes in life you have to make a change in order for something different to happen. Sometimes if you change an attitude about something, life will get easier. Other times you have to replace a bad habit for a better habit or get out of an abusive situation.

Go for help, make a phone call or go to a shelter, but do it now before things get worse. Never give up - there is always someone out there who can help. Sometimes people have to change their lives, their houses, or jobs, or spouses or relationships. Or they have to confront something. Pray for wisdom, and make the change. Have faith and ask a higher power to help you. Co-create with Spirit, and you will be a mighty force.

A Serenade, or Retrograde

Sometimes illness can be cured and problems are lightweight,
Other times more serious and with much more difficult fates.
A cold or flu can be worked through, but how about cancer,
heart attacks, or AIDS.
Sometimes life is a serenade, and other times goes retrograde.
When storms are brewing, there is no use in stewing,
find a peaceful way.
If you have faith it is God's world, you find peace when you pray.

Travesty of Justice

In the courts - if a travesty of justice makes some things hard to accept,
Or if evil seems to be dismissed, still we should not forget.
A person's merits will be decided someday in the celestial stars.
Good and evil will be divided in those heavenly charts, from afar.

Why Marriage?

Some Say, Why Marriage?
Some say it is just a piece of paper, full of vapor,
But that is not true.
It may seem like vapor, but is written in the stars beyond,
A deep and celestial bond.

Vive La Difference

Men's emotions go back and forth, women's go up and down.
So is it any wonder if we can ever find a common ground?
Our love can flourish like two flowers,
If showing emotions to each other waters them.
We fertilize our bonds with understanding,
If we are real and don't pretend.

Sometimes we go through most unpredictable weather,
Pull many, many weeds out, and yet we still can be together.
We cultivate with passion, honesty, trust and love,
And are often helped by Spirit from Above.

Divorce

Sometimes people stay to grow, but other times leave to save their soul.
Sometimes humans are afraid, with the decision which they made.
Through a river of tears and a breaking heart,
sometimes people have to part.
Oil and water cannot mix, some situations can't be fixed.
Remember the good - let go of the bad - rejoice in the good times
you have had.

Second Families

Sometimes there is no acceptance in a second family. I know a woman who says for her own peace of mind she stays away from her spouse's family. She tried to get them to accept her but it did not work. However, she keeps herself positive, enjoying her husband and their life together. There is no doubt that blended or second families can sometimes be difficult, especially when it comes to defining boundaries. But always - change what you can, let the rest go, and your soul will grow.

Nursing Home Visits

Life can be lonely for the elderly. Visit them. Talk to them. I used to work in a nursing home and noticed that few people would come to visit. It does not matter if they hear every word or remember the things you say. It does matter that you took the time to visit. Perhaps they are aware just at that moment you are there in front of them, and that moment is a blessing for them. Let the residents tell their old stories even if you have heard them before. Bring the kids. It brings happiness into their day. Or bring an animal if possible - both the animals and nursing home residents love this. Play cards or read to them. Don't stay away because of conflicts or because facing your own mortality may be difficult. Just love them. Pat their hand or kiss their cheek, or smooth their hair and try to share. Somehow deep down in their souls they are aware of your kindness.

Nine-One-One, the Wake Up Call

As an immigrant from Sweden when he was just nine years old,
My father was one of many with a story to be told.
Standing on the boat in New York Harbor when he first arrived,
Excited and exhilarated, he stood there and he cried.
As he first viewed our lady and the statue of our liberty,
This symbol of America was standing so majestically.

America is a land of such a positive free power,
Yet was taken such advantage of on that dark September hour.
This horrendous shocking day, on the eleventh of September,
Is etched forever in our minds and we will long remember.
Humanity was threatened by a catastrophic nine-one-one.
This appalling wake-up call was here for each and everyone.

America was attacked, and we so quickly lost so many lives.
How fragile this dear world can be, we start to realize.
Yet stories drifted in, amid the pain and dreadful shock,
America reeled in horror and yet we started to take stock.
The showing of humanity, no matter what the color or creed
Was magnificent to know about and so hopeful indeed.

The Firefighters, Police, and all the Rescue Workers on the Force
Were helping this disaster as they soothed the tragic course.
Our brave American heroes on the planes so beautifully
Showed the Spirit of our nation for the entire world to see.
We forever mourn and won't forget; yet we go on with courage.
We now do face a less safe world, but should not get discouraged.

Instead, direct our anger in a positive good way,
Asking God for guidance, we remember first to pray.
Our children need to know we must be strong and most resilient.
We must be spiritual warriors, most alert and diligent.
We can't assume our freedoms as our lives are rearranged,
And can't afford to be complacent as our lives are changed.

Yet, we will not be paralyzed in the dark of night,
America will persevere and beam her shining light.
America grew up that day, the eleventh of September.
Not so naive or trusting, yet good values we remember.
New courage will inspire us as we still have our kind hearts,
Yet we aren't afraid to stand our ground, as we do our own part.

Our children need to learn from us the truths that keep us strong.
There are lessons in our lives, of what is right and what is wrong.
We must rebuild together and we must communicate.
Each one of us is needed as together we relate.
Our courage will inspire us - also truth, honor, and love,
And I think that we are truly helped by Spirit from above.

But There Was September 10th

On September 10th, the day before this disaster, I taught an angel class at White Bear, Minnesota at the Metaphysical Emporium. There were eight women with me that night and one of them had had a kidney operation two weeks prior to this class. She sat in a corner of the classroom that night listening, and I kept walking over to her to give her handouts for the class. At the end of the hour, I had her stand with the rest of us in a circle and we all prayed for her quick recovery. I felt the angels that night and I believe the others in the class did too. About a month later this woman's sister came into our store and said the doctors were amazed over her quick recovery. I believe the angels were very busy that night, helping us to heal this woman.

In spite of the terrible tragedy of this disaster on September 11th, I still remember September 10th, and the power of this group of women in my class and their angels who were with us that night. I still believe the good overpowers the bad - always!

Many Storms of Life

There are many, many storms in life, but in weathering these storms one should remember that the past cannot be changed. Let it go and change the future. There are many, many storms that bring hard lessons but after the storm there is cleansing and renewal once again. Even though there are thorns on a rose, there is still the marvelous beauty of the rose, and likewise there are positive things to find in life, making it all worthwhile.

10
Celebrations of Life

Pierre's Philosophy

When I was ten years old, my pet mom decided I needed a birthday party so she bought streamers and birthday hats. She bought cake and ice cream for my human guests and tuna for me. The guests were adolescent friends of her youngest son, who by now was the only child still living at the house.

One of the lessons animals can teach people is simply to have fun and to play. When I was younger I liked to play catch - cats are just as bright and capable of playing catch as dogs are but often we just don't feel like it. We are very independent and may seem a bit aloof, but of course that is just a facade. We

Pierre's Birthday Party

really care about everything. And once in a while it is fun to play catch!

My Favorite Toy

My pet mom had a red fuzzy ball that came off of some fringe she used for one of her artistic projects (sometimes I don't understand why humans waste so much time working on projects when they could be taking a nice catnap). I did like to chase that fringe ball.

She would sit in the living room and toss the ball down the steps of our two-story house. I would chase after it, usually catching it on the landing, retrieve it and bring it back to her. Then I would sit down by the ball and wait expectantly for her to throw it again. The only trouble was that I was doing all of the work. After a while this got boring, so I would pretend to be unable to find the ball to return it. I would try to abscond with this fuzzy thing and eat it fast but she always caught me. Humans are sometimes smarter than they appear.

Celebrate life and play sometimes; this is a good thing to do. My pet parents seem to understand this concept and enjoy each day, whether it is rainy or sunny. If the sun is not shining and I cannot find choice nap spots, I sit under a lamp where at least it is bright and warm. I have found as I get older, I like to sleep under warm blankets or under my pet mom's robe as it is nice and cozy there.

Another way to celebrate life is to groom oneself. Any cat knows this. Dogs don't seem to care, but grooming is important and makes one feel good. My owner brushes me a lot more than she used to. She realizes that sometimes I get tired - after all I am an older cat. It is hard to keep up the high standards I have always had for myself! When she brushes me, it feels like a nice massage and is very soothing.

Karla's Celestial Thoughts

Pierre taught me how to celebrate. He is always here in the moment, appreciating being alive. There are so many occasions when one can celebrate!

The New Millennium

On New Year's Eve in 1999, our family drove into St. Paul and walked the streets in the middle of the night. It was about ten degrees below zero, rather chilly even for sturdy Minnesotans! We watched a parade led by a huge dragon float and then we danced the night away with some people who were dressed in frog costumes, and who were just plain happy! At midnight we watched a fireworks display that sprayed rainbow patterns over the Mississippi River. It was a beautiful sight, with sparkling, bursting colors. A new millennium was upon us, bringing much new energy.

The Valentine Lady

I have a sister-in-law who was once crowned queen of the University of Minnesota Homecoming Pageant. She has always been the "Queen of Hearts" to me. It is natural that she was born on Valentine's Day.

Sadly, her eldest son became ill with hepatitis and died when he was only in his twenties. After his passing, we inherited his 12 foot high tin knight that we placed down by the shore where it could look out over the lake. We call it the Guardian of the Lake.

One year on my sister-in-law's birthday, I was standing in the living room gazing out the bay window at the icy lake beyond. It was a snowy day and the snow on our landing outside had turned to ice, sticking to the tops of the railing all along the porch. One of these piled up icy spots on top of the landing had a hole in the ice, and I noticed this hole was shaped like a heart.

My heart leapt as I thought of my sister-in-law, knowing this was her birthday but more than that, it was a very special moment as I felt her eldest son was communicating with me through Spirit. Looking through the heart shaped hole in the ice, the trajectory was perfectly in line with the knight down by the lake. It gave me chills, and I called my sister-in-law to give her his message.

St. Patrick's Day

I always think of a dear friend of mine on St. Patrick's Day as we usually meet on that night to celebrate, wearing green, and find an establishment where Irish music is played. It is a difficult night for my friend to celebrate because her mom died on that evening years ago.

One St. Patrick's Day evening there were wonderful snowflakes falling, which we called 'shamrock snowflakes' because they were the hugest flakes I have ever seen. It was a very dramatic storm. We gazed out of the window that night remembering the life of my friend's mom and all the gifts she had brought to the family. No matter what disaster a person might have been going through, her response was always the same: "Well, if that is the worst thing that is happening to you," she would say, "it is not so bad." She always looked at the world with a positive heart.

She died on St. Patrick's Day so I think of that day in a bittersweet way, remembering her, and yet knowing she would want us to be happy and to go on celebrating with joy in our hearts.

Easter Shadows

One Easter morning when I was a child, we were going to a Lutheran Church to attend a service. As we were leaving the house my dad said, "Karla, notice that shadow on the wall. Do not think these things are just coincidence, because what people call coincidences often have meanings and hidden messages."

There on the wall in the dining room was a perfect little cross caused by the sunlight hitting the wall through the windowpane in a certain way. I looked up at my dad and smiled at him. He smiled back at me with understanding.

Waters Calmed on Easter Morning

One year when I was young we were in St. Petersburg, Florida for Easter. It was a calm, quiet, beautiful Easter morning when my dad woke us up and told us to come down to the ocean for a minute. The ocean was without a ripple or wave on it, perfectly still. It was like a huge, bluish sparkling mirror. It was the most improbable sight and I have never witnessed such a thing before or since that special miracle of Easter. The calm, the warmth, the sun on the smooth waters and my dad saying, "well kids, Happy Easter," will forever remain imprinted in my memory.

Galactic Easter at the St. Paul Cathedral

One year, I went to an Easter mass with some teenage friends of my youngest son. As I prayed quietly, I kept getting the sense that Christ is a cosmic Christ, a universal Christ. The longer I meditated on this idea, the more it solidified in my mind. When I opened my eyes and looked up at the ceiling, I felt the energies of other worlds, other planets and a vortex opening for me, like a portal in the ceiling of the cathedral. Another dimension was opening up!

I sensed there was a giant spaceship with many lights shining from it right above us and I thought again of Christ as a much more universal, cosmic Christ, and even extraterrestrial.

After mass, we drove to a new age bookstore downtown and as soon as we walked into the store, I was compelled to go over to a certain section. My hand was heating up near a particular book so I pulled it off the shelf. When I opened it, the page read, "Christ, as a Cosmic Christ."

At that time there were very few books written on this subject, although now one can find many more. Needless to say, I had a very cosmic Easter that year!

Pierre the Easter Cat

A Rare, Beautiful Gift on Mother's Day

I once received a special gift from my son, Forrest, who is not usually a gift giver. He has gotten a lot of mileage out of this gift, for years and years.

Our kids were all hungry teenagers as they sat at the breakfast table on Sunday, waiting for my Swedish pancakes. I had two griddles going at once; these kids ate a lot, and quickly! Everyone asked to be excused when they were done, except for my eldest son who was still hanging around when I finally sat down to eat my own pancakes. When I looked up, I saw a vase in the middle of the table filled with a dozen beautiful, red roses! Being a busy mother, I had not noticed them, although I did feel like something was "in the air." I looked over at my son, realizing he had given them to me, and quickly swept him into an embrace, not concerned whether he got embarrassed or not!

A Message from the Sky on Father's Day

The last Father's Day my dad was alive was in 1969, and I will never forget it. Joe and I were helping him to build a dock at the lake that summer. As we worked, a small plane flew overhead, then landed at a little airport not far away. Five people had parachuted out of the airplane and as they were drifting down to their designated landing site, my dad got an odd look on his face and said, "You know, those look sort of like angels dropping from the sky."

I got chills when he said that as it was such an unusual thing for him to say, and I often wondered later if he'd had a premonition. He died two weeks later of a heart attack.

Fourth of July, New Perspectives

My grandfather, dad, brother and nephew are, or were, all architects. Eventually, my dad took a position as an executive engineer at 3M where he worked for many years. I have always been interested in the architecture of different buildings, I think because of my relatives making me aware of the beauty in creating houses. To me, architecture is another form of art.

Dad had designed and worked on building our lake cabin himself, a labor of love, and it was finally completed the summer I was nine years old. It was finished a week before the Fourth of July, and so on Independence Day our entire family climbed the long ladder to our roof and watched the fireworks going off in a small town three miles away. We were delighted with the beautiful, exploding display. It was fascinating to watch the fireworks from the top of a roof.

This was one of my favorite Fourth of July celebration memories, as a nine year old girl sitting atop our new cabin by the lake.

Halloween Costumes

I always made costumes for our kids on Halloween. I also had my own costume - enjoying an excuse to dress up and play with the kids. We did not have neighbors so had to drive around for candy, although we usually only went to six or seven places. We really enjoy celebrations in our family. If it was a birthday party, we had streamers, party hats and cake. Just like when we celebrated Pierre's birthdays.

Now, years later I have gone to Star Trek and Xena conventions with my eldest daughter, both of us wearing costumes. Many people are afraid to put themselves out there and take a risk, but why not? They might have fun!

It was Trekkie heaven this past year with my daughter, as we wore our homemade costumes to the annual convention in Minneapolis. She played

Our kids in Halloween costumes

Elaan of Troilus, an empowered, strong female character, and I was a blue-faced Andorian, with antennas on my head. Getting into the spirit of celebrations and wearing costumes can be a very joyful experience and I believe more people should be open to expressing themselves more freely, having fun in this and other ways.

Thanksgiving Blessings

I always count my blessings at Thanksgiving - having a good family and being happy are precious gifts. This year I am especially thankful as we still have our Pierre, the best cat in the world. It is always the time of reflections, memories, and appreciation of what one has in life. Animals are big blessings.

The Live Nativity

When our children were young, we bundled them up in their snowsuits on Christmas night and took them with us to see a live nativity at a church in our small town. There was a wonderful procession with wise men coming to see Mary and Joseph and the baby, and they used a real donkey, cow and lamb in the show! It was impressive and realistic and we were enthralled. It was very cold that night as we stood in the snow, huddled together, quietly watching the performance. All three of the animals were so well behaved, as if they knew this was a reverent moment.

As we walked silently back to our car at the end of the performance, Joe said to our kids, "Now that is the true meaning of Christmas."

The Solstices and Equinoxes

I have started celebrating these magical times, doing rituals in the labyrinth I made in our woods. Labyrinths are a marvelous way to be connected with the Spirit.

The **Winter Solstice** in mid-December is the shortest day of the year, and the longest night. This is a time of inner spiritual reflection and celebration.

The **Spring Equinox** in mid-March is when the day and night are of equal length, and a time of renewal and faith. With spring comes new energy.

The **Summer Solstice** in mid-June is the longest day of the year and the shortest night, and a time to celebrate the blooming of the trees, flowers, and greenery.

The **Autumn Equinox** in mid-September is a time when we have a harvest, and appreciation of our bountiful blessings in life, and again equal time of day and night.

Four Seasons

Small miracles are born each hour - the budding beauty of a flower.
Exquisite butterflies in flight - a golden sunset, stars at night.
With gentle love God does create what we should all appreciate,
As nature stoops to rearrange, in ways mysterious and strange.

Soft magic greets us every spring, God's harmony in everything.
The birds return, in patterns led, and spring's first robin bobs its head.
The lilacs with their fragrance dear, fresh pussy willows with their cheer.
Such fragile beauty fills the air, created with such loving care.

Each year in spring new thoughts intrude - rush on to shake our solitude.
We pause to listen to our hearts - of this grand world we all are part.
My soul rejoices every spring, as I feel love in everything.
And with a faith I feel renewed - my favorite time of year ensues.

*   *   *   *

Summertime and lotus lilies, toads are hopping, acting silly.
Sunshine days and blessed hours, flowers blooming with their power.
A turtle on the sandy road, cicadas sing the songs they know.
A beaver, rabbit, mourning dove - awakened nature brings such love.

The sun is shining way up high - a warm, bright beacon in the sky.
The trees and grasses finally green as nature's beauty now is seen.
Soft and gentle breezes play, melodic messages each day.
And all of the earth does burst with pride, the world awakened,
far and wide.

*   *   *   *

Reds and oranges, golds and browns, many leaves come tumbling down.
This is fall and harvest time, with leaves dressed up in colors, fine.
A north wind blows as seasons shift, and slowly falling leaves do drift.
Leaves dance before they touch the ground, as they leap and swirl around.

This time of year is sometimes sad, we reminisce on times we had.
And yet it is invigorating, and sometimes most exhilarating.
In autumn we may come to life, with brand new goals within our sight.
And nature has her final hour, gathering crops within her power.

*   *   *   *

Soft enchantment fills the air, as snowflakes appear everywhere.
All seasons bring unique designs, as nature's beauty intertwines.
In winter we sometimes will regroup, and somehow we may then recoup.
Nature is dormant for a time, for that is nature's own design.

If Christmas lives within our heart, we find in life we have a part.
Peace and love we should hold dear; this is time we should revere.
And the entire world renews next spring, bringing new life to everything.
Our lives are important and most unique -
through many voices we may speak.

*   *   *   *

All the seasons can bring pleasures, as they each have their own treasures.
Spring and summer, fall and winter - always a new world to enter.
Let us learn and let us grow, as we do expand our souls.
And if we live life with great heart, we co-create and do our part.

*   *   *   *

Walking in the Deep of Winter

The Sun is shining with her dazzling fire.
In the winter she is up for a few short hours, then quietly retires.
The Wind is dancing, with cool moving air.
Caressing the earth with her loving care.
The Snow has melted and returned to water now.
She loves to change her ways, as only she knows how.

The fourth element, the Earth, seems dormant, yet she has a plan
Although one we may not understand.
Earth is forever beautiful, lest we do forget.
Her die is cast, her purpose here is set.

I feel the dirt beneath my feet as I walk along.
Being out in nature, Earth's energies are strong.
I feel so much a part of life,
Everything will be all right.

Wispy clouds in white and gray,
Also have their say.
All shapes and sizes move along,
Telling their own story, singing their own song.

Life, like clouds, can look gray and dark, or look white and clear.
We find a faith in life, or we live in fear.

We need the storms and darkness, as we live through rain and snow.
We need precipitation so we all can grow.
The trees are there, greeting me with their vibrations.
As they have their conversations.

The Birch tree says, "I bring purity and love."
Meanwhile the Pine tree sighs with soft peacefulness,
Swaying in the breeze.
The Oak is patient with great wisdom,
And the unassuming Ash tree says, "Also, look at me."

Nature lies dormant in December,
Yet it is a time to remember.
Next spring will happen, do not fear,
Bringing renewal and great cheer.
And so the elements are gathered together,
Discussing this most wintery weather.

Sun says, "I'm much cooler than in summer, but I can still smile."
Wind says, "I stop my harsh breezes once in awhile."
Snow says, "There are times in the winter when I will melt."
Earth says, "Hope for springtime, in the dead of winter, still can be felt."

In their own way the elements always bring us hope,
Helping in dark wintery hours to cope.
Spring will come, spring will come - yes, it will return.
And so I tramp with joyful steps, as I think and yearn.

Count your blessings and be glad to be here. Cancer patients or
people who are very ill or old can understand why one should appreciate
every minute of being alive. I celebrate many things - starting a job,
leaving a job, solstices, a promotion, finishing a project, the full moon,
the new moon, creating a painting or any art project, building a house,
retiring or starting a business. There are a million things to celebrate
every year, big and small. So celebrate life whenever you have the
opportunity. Live in the moment. Be mindful and be positive.

11
Zodiac Garden in the Sky

Pierre's Philosophy

Just as the moon affects the tides of the ocean, so also do the planets and stars affect this world. I am a star cat, aware of the zodiac constellations in the sky. The sun guides us in the daytime and the moon guides us at night. Purrrrfect heavenly bodies. To me the concept of astrology is quite simple.

My pet family has all of the astrological elements covered. The three women in the family are water signs. My pet dad is an earth sign and the two sons are fire and air, respectively.

As an Aries, I am a pioneer for the animals, breaking through

Celestial Light

barriers and bringing new knowledge and ideas to the world through my pet mom after all these many years.

◊　**Aries** can be a ram that is brave, bold, and airy. Courageous animals and creatures, they don't mind butting heads with someone. They are bold and energetic, swooping down as a bird, wiggling as a fish, or slinking away quickly like a snake.

◊ **Taurus** are sometimes bullying and determined, and not afraid to get into the mud. The animals and people born under the influence of this sign are grounded and strong. They also can be slow moving, and wish to be comfortable in whatever they do.

◊ **Gemini** are talkers, barkers, meowers, and good communicators. They often like to talk at very high speed.

◊ **Cancers** are feeling, loving, caring crabs, and like to be with family.

◊ **Leos** can shine with a roar of pride, like a lion. They often like to be in the limelight.

◊ **Virgos** like to have order in their lives. They strive to be neat, like ants in a colony. They are organizers, and like to help the world.

◊ **Libras** like beauty and balance. I picture the pink flamingo balancing on one leg in the shallows in a stream when I think of them.

◊ **Scorpios** are very intense and can sting like a scorpion, yet they are also deeply caring.

◊ **Sagittarius** want to help other creatures with a higher purpose, running swiftly forward like the centaur.

◊ **Capricorn**, the goat, can stand alone on a mountain, and yet not be lonely.

◊ **Aquarius** likes to do things in a different way, not like everyone else, and likes to be free with fresh thoughts, hopes, and ideas. They like to be in crowds, with other critters.

◊ **Pisces** can be a fish which either swims upstream fighting things, or goes with the flow, often changeable.

Karla's Celestial Thoughts

Zodiac Garden, a Campfire in the Sky

I dreamed of a campfire in the sky. All of the star signs were sitting around the campfire, which was on a huge, white, ethereal cloud. With a burst of energy, the red planet Mars rolled across the heavens to sit behind the first star sign, the ram Aries who said, "I am just bursting with energies and want to develop my personality. I can do it myself. I am impatient and unafraid to take on the world. It is springtime in this garden, and I am fresh with new ideas and warmth."

From behind Aries, Mars smiled with a fiery grin at the ram's enthusiasm. He wisely said, "Yes, but your lesson is to have tact and to share, bringing others with you on our journey in the sky. Share with others your PURITY OF PURPOSE."

The ram snorted hard but he did listen well and said in his hearty voice, "Oh, I shall. I am a pioneer and I can learn. Thank you, Mars." And the ram trotted over to see Venus, telling her to go to the second sign and sit behind Taurus the bull. The ram accompanied her so that he could also listen, although he first informed the bull that he would try to cooperate with him and become more patient.

Venus sat behind the bull Taurus, sending love and affection to him. and the bull said, "I am figuring out the material world. It is later in the spring in this garden in the sky and I am slow and steady in the world, and a hard worker."

From behind him Venus wisely said, "Yes, but your lesson is to have more positive thoughts and to not be so unbending. Loosen up a bit."

The bull said, "hummmmmmmmph."

However, he listened and ran over to see the next sign, Gemini. The twin stars sat together at the fire and he told the twins he would work with them to learn UNSELFISHNESS from others.

Mercury then rolled over to sit behind the twins, Gemini and the two stars spoke at once, saying in unison, "We wish to communicate and are very lively and always curious about life. Spring is here, it is in full force."

Mercury spoke to the twins, saying, "You need to learn to be tranquil and have FOCUS." The twins looked at each other and nodded, although one twin had an easier time understanding than the other, as both sides of this sign can sometimes be at odds. They turned to the next star sign, Cancer the crab, and told him together they were going to be very open and work with him, always in a calm, passive way.

Next, the Moon came to sit behind the next star sign, Cancer, the crab. It was now the beginning of summer, a time of year when everything is in bloom. As we moved through the zodiac in the sky, we were now at the Summer Solstice. The crab was emotional and said he loved the importance of home and family in the world.

The Moon spoke to him saying, "You are very sensitive and kind but need to learn to have faith in yourself and face life with SELF-CONFIDENCE. Stop walking sideways sometimes, and face things. Walk forward." The crab listened well and agreed with the Moon, turning to the next sign sitting in the circle, Leo the lion. The crab told the lion he now believed in himself and wished to communicate with him.

The Sun came up to sit behind Leo and now the warmth of the summer garden in the sky was at its height. The lion said, "I am proud of myself and have enthusiasm and strong ideas and opinions about things."

The Sun told him, "Yes, but you need to learn to SHARE THE POWER with the world. Let the world shine with you." And so Leo turned to the next sign, Virgo the swan. Leo told the swan he would try to work with him but not over him.

Mercury moved over from the twins and came to sit behind the swan. Virgo, the swan spoke up to the circle sitting around the campfire, saying, "I am efficient and neat and logical, why can't more people see my scientific and logical way of looking at things?"

Mercury spoke from behind him, saying, "It is the time of summer harvest and you need to learn to appreciate the riches of the earth without trying to control them. You need a BROADER OUTLOOK in your work and in life in general."

The swan listened and agreed and ran over to the seventh sign, Libra the zebra.

Now Venus moved over from the bull and sat behind the zebra. The zebra said, "I am easygoing in life, I like beautiful things and I weigh everything before I make waves of any sort as I see many sides to things and I see some things as black and others as white."

Venus, a symbol of love, said to the zebra, "Yes, but you need to learn to be more decisive, take a chance, and MAKE DECISIONS."

The zebra listened intently and turned to the next sign, as autumn was in the air in this celestial garden in the sky. He told Scorpio the scorpion that he would like to work with her. Pluto came to sit at the campfire behind Scorpio. It was now autumn in the garden and the flowers were fading.

In an extremely intense voice Scorpio said, "I am discerning about things in life and feel very passionate about things. I am very determined."

Pluto replied in turn, "Yes, but please listen to me, you need to learn TOLERANCE of yourself and others. Listen up." Reluctantly the scorpion agreed, this was most likely true, and she scooted over to the next star sign, Sagittarius the archer, telling him she would try to work with him and his talents.

Great big Jupiter rolled in to sit behind Sagittarius with a mighty roar. It was now winter and rather cold in the garden. The centaur, man-horse said, "I am adventurous and I like to do things. I like change and am restless but clever and dependable."

Jupiter said to Sagittarius, "But you need to learn SELF DISCIPLINE and patience." And so the centaur snorted, yet listened well and turned to the tenth zodiac sign in the sky, the Capricorn. He communicated that he, the centaur, would try to learn more discipline.

Saturn charged in to sit behind the goat in the sky. This was in the dark of winter now, the time of the Winter Solstice. Capricorn the goat spoke to the group, saying, "I am self-disciplined and a loner and opinionated, that is simply the way I am."

Saturn had lots of patience, and he said to Capricorn, "But you need to be more FORGIVING and loosen up a bit." and so the goat sighed but he did move closer to the next sign, Aquarius, which was represented by a little waterfall. He told the group that he would try to be more yielding and loosen up.

Uranus rolled in from the sky to sit behind the waterfall. Aquarius then said, "I am bright and loyal and interested in life, and also frank and open. What could I possibly have to learn? But like the other signs in the sky, he did have a lesson or two to learn.

With great gentleness Uranus said, "It is winter now, but leaning towards spring in the celestial garden. You need to thaw out and BE LESS FIXED in your opinions, of which you have many, and take chances in life." And so, Aquarius moved over to the next star sign Pisces, the two fish, and the last sign in the zodiac. He told both of the fish he wished to be open to them and maybe learn something new from them.

In came Neptune, eager to sit behind the two fish at the campfire in the sky. Spring was coming again to the garden and the Spring Equinox along with it, bringing change. The twelfth of the star signs was connected to all of the other signs, representing a rich and complex tapestry of energy created by the combination of the full zodiac.

Pisces, the two fish, spoke together. "We are kind and nurturing, sympathetic, adaptable, humble and receptive."

Yes," said Neptune, "But you need to learn to help others in the world in the right way. Be caring, but don't interfere with other creatures of the world. You tune into other worlds but have to live in this one, so straighten up and APPLY YOURSELF." The two fish looked at each other after hearing this speech from Neptune and then wiggled over to the first sign, Aries, and expressed their wish to learn from this sign, thus completing the circle.

All of the sun signs held hands, fins, paws, hooves, or whatever they could to create a chain around the campfire in the sky and send their blessings of love and peace to each other and to the whole world. They promised to all work together in unison, each bringing their own gifts to the garden of life.

When I awakened from this fabulous dream I was stunned by the powerful messages I had been given. I believe we can learn many lessons from astrology about how we can improve our lives, and when we study our own individual star charts it makes it so much easier to understand why we are the way we are and to open up to the possibilities in our lives. We look into this ancient system to understand ourselves.

12
Polar Bears and Teddy Bears

Pierre's Philosophy

I always know when my pet mom is coming home. I sit up on the staircase watching the front door for about a half an hour before she returns. Preparing for our reunion is a special time. Imagine how you feel when you know a loved one is returning home, and perhaps you too have had the experience of "knowing" when someone was coming. We know when our human families are coming home. We can feel them. It is always a wonderful reunion of human/animal bonding.

Here is another pet time story my pet mom told me one night as I sat on her lap. It is about the time she and my pet dad decided to visit the Duluth Zoo on the way home from their cabin. They had not been there for quite a few years and were wondering if anything interesting had been added to the facility. The zoo had been expanded to include larger quarters and a larger variety of animals.

My pet parents became intrigued by two polar bears who were playing "catch" with a large white bucket that people threw out to them in the water. The bears would gracefully balance on their hind legs in the water as they pranced up and down on their feet. At the same time they used their nose and front paws to get a grip on the bucket and then they would throw the bucket back out of the water for the people to toss back down to them again. Both species, human and animal, were communicating for no other reason than the pure pleasure of playing together. The bears were not being fed in order to perform; they were just doing it for fun. On that joyful, sunny autumn day the humans and bears were playing together as friends.

Interspecies Communication

My pet mom went to lunch with a friend and noticed that a gorgeous South American fish weighing about twelve pounds was swimming in a fish tank in the restaurant. Nina the fish seemed to either greet people in a positive or negative way when they went up to her tank. She was very discriminating. If she didn't like certain people she would splash with her fins to keep away from them, but for the people she did like she would swim up to the surface and happily wiggle her tail.

My pet mom interrupted her lunch to go up to Nina's tank because she just had to visit this extraordinary fish! Lori, the restaurant owner, said that if Nina really liked a person she would act as if she wanted to be petted, and she especially liked being petted by a friend. A person could put a hand in the tank and Nina would approach, waiting to be stroked. My pet mom petted her that day, enjoying the communication.

Karla's Celestial Thoughts

One Hundred Hamsters Came to Light

One hundred hamsters came to light in the middle of the night.
They were in cages everywhere, a rather frightening sight.
My mom said my brother could raise just a few alone,
But what she did not realize is how many he brought home.

For, somehow they had multiplied, and multiplied again,
And here in a brief time it seemed there were many more than ten.
Their kids had kids and grand-kids, and we noticed pretty soon,
My brother could not keep count, and there wasn't any room.

One day, my mom could stand no more - she had simply reached her limit.
My brother made another cage and she wished that he was in it.

And so the hamsters were soon sold or else given away.
Our mom rejoiced and skipped a bit on that most happy day.

The lesson of the story is the patience of a mother,
And learning of responsibility, which you did, dear brother.
Now, if you ever get a pet be sure to know its habits,
Or someday you may find they all will multiply like rabbits!

Monarchs of Gold

The last autumn I was able to spend with my mother before she passed away was a cherished time. One day in particular stands out in my memory. My kids and I were sitting on her back porch at her lake cabin when we noticed Monarch butterflies were flying towards the neighbor's trees near the lake. It seemed like we were witnessing a host of orange and black angels or fairies dressed in ornate attire having one last autumn ball. We watched as they landed under a huge willow tree by the water.

Mom admired them, then turned to me and said, "Isn't this beautiful, Karla? Remember the gifts of nature; don't ever forget them. They surround us every day."

My Dad said almost the same thing when I was fishing with him many years earlier. In the angel cards I created, butterflies represent rebirth and new joy, the recycling of life.

Comfort from Precious Friends

I can clearly recall two consecutive Easters when I was quite young and my parents gave us toy bunnies in our Easter baskets. Because I loved stuffed animals so much, my brother and sister eventually gave their bunnies to me. I slept with three of them on one side of me and three along my other side. I was lined from head to toe in bunnies, feeling like they were my protectors. I felt very comforted.

When I later married and had children of my own, I continued this idea of giving stuffed toy animals for presents. Over the years, our kids had a real menagerie. When our children were really young they each had a toy monkey with which they acted out their adventures.

The kids would often use empty tissue boxes for pretend go-carts, which they raced around on the floor playing bumper cars.

One year, Hazel had pneumonia, and I made her a panda bear companion to help her feel better. It cheered her up tremendously. Though it was a challenge to find the time to make this special gift when I was so busy with raising four young kids, I was so grateful I made the effort. The instant comfort this handmade bear brought was obvious. Hazel held it and talked to it and slept with it practically pinned to her side as she recuperated.

Hazel and her panda

When in Doubt, Use a Toy

Years later, when I worked in a group home for the handicapped, I was better able to talk with a woman who had Down's Syndrome when she held her toy dog. It was an instant comfort to her. Similarly, when I worked at a nursing home, there was a woman who would converse openly with me when she was holding a toy doll in her lap. Without the doll she was afraid to speak up to anyone. When we feel alone and isolated it is important to find some way to connect. Often it is easier to trust things than to trust people, especially when we feel vulnerable.

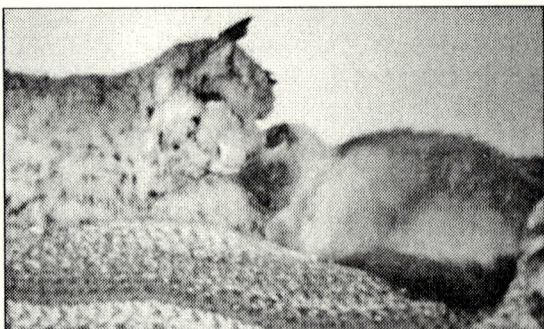

Pierre being comforted

I have a friend who is a counselor and she told me that in her office there is a bin of toy animals and dolls she invites her clients to use. Holding soft things that remind them of childhood comfort helps her clients find the courage to address the difficult issues they are working with in therapy.

13
ET's and Other Worlds

Pierre's Philosophy

While writing this book, my pet mom told me about a sweat lodge ceremony from which she had just returned (another pet time story). When I found out what one of my animal sisters did in the ceremony, I was so proud! She was a dog - a huge, calm, peaceful black Rottweiler named Sheila. Sheila was the caretaker of the ceremony and guardian of the sweat lodge. She allowed good spirits in but kept out the bad ones. She patrolled around the tent being very vigilant.

This dog had deep wisdom in her eyes. From the minute my pet mom met her she knew there was something very special about her. She was strong and powerful, almost like an angel, protecting with an inner force, not just with her brawn. My pet mom had many flashbacks to her Indian lives as she sat in the sweat lodge. The Indians are also very connected to the space people - the extraterrestrials. They reach out in Spirit to other dimensions.

As red-hot rocks were carried from outside the canvas tent into the center pit of the sweat lodge, each rock took on characteristics of other beings. My pet mom saw many images as she looked at the rocks. The first time they were added from the outside pit to the pit inside the tent, she viewed a small extraterrestrial being in the glowing red rock. Four times, representing the four winds, these rocks were brought in as part of the ceremony and ritual. The last time the rocks came in, Sheila started howling.

Something was about to occur. It was a rare evening with many higher dimensions coming in. Then suddenly, the lid blew off the top of the sweat lodge, surprising everyone in the tent. This had never happened before! Two of the participants crawled out of the tent to repair the damage. My pet mom said the feeling of the group seemed to reach a new higher level, and everyone agreed that it was a most unusual night.

Karla's Celestial Thoughts

Mary's Intuitive Classes

In Mary's class we often prayed or meditated together as a group and I started to see and feel the presence of the strangest thing yet - *Star People*. I kept seeing joyful, happy green beings from another dimension, although I knew it seemed quite crazy. One night they came into my consciousness again and I saw a group of these little guys dragging a huge piece of paper across the room on which they had written the word MULLOCK. I felt they were attempting to tell me their collective name. I knew they were some kind of Star People from another dimension but I doubted I should say anything to anyone, as it just seemed too odd.

One night Mary was channeling when all of a sudden her whole demeanor changed quite dramatically. Mary raised one of her arms very high as she said in a deep booming voice,

"GREETINGS EARTHLINGS!"

Her whole face seemed to change right in front of us and her mannerisms were entirely different than usual. If I had not seen it myself I probably never would have believed any of it, (although since then I have come to know channeling works, and have learned to do it myself, privately).

I quickly grabbed a pad and pencil so I could write down what Mary was saying.

"YOU ARE THE PEOPLE OF THE LIGHT AND IT IS GOOD YOU ARE SEARCHING FOR TRUTHS. YOU MUST LOVE AND HELP OTHERS TO SEE THE LIGHT. I HAVE BEEN ON YOUR PLANET FOR TEN YEARS AND GOOD CHANGES ARE COMING, MUCH GROWTH, THROUGH PEOPLE LIKE YOU."

Someone asked where this ET was from and Mary said from the star Sirius. We asked Mary many more questions that she answered in a booming voice as she continued channeling.

Then I asked, "Have you ever heard of the Star People, Mullocks?"

She drew back as if she was startled, and then said, "YES, I KNOW OF THEM, BUT THEY ARE FROM ANOTHER STAR SYSTEM THAN MINE. THEY ARE LOVING, KIND AND GENTLE CREATURES."

I was excited to have my strange experiences with the Star People validated in this way.

A few weeks after this unusual channeling at Mary's house, a friend told me about a book called *The Mayan Factor*. On page 100, he discovered information about extraterrestrials and found a race called "the Mullucs" mentioned! They were supposed to have been a race developed to awaken the consciousness of the human race. The similarity was startling, and I was delighted to have this affirmation.

Mary told me there would be a lot of doubters in the world until people had their own experience with something unusual happening and then maybe they would begin to believe.

The Gathering

I had a powerful experience in Los Angeles at a large psychic store years ago. My nephew, whom I had been visiting, dropped me at this store knowing I would be

Eric's charcoal drawings

intrigued with it. The store was very crowded but I immediately found my way to the New Age section, although I had not been in that store before. This is normal for me, as I usually do this in stores, and often when I find a book I should buy it will heat up in my hand. I had heard of the book *Star People* and wanted to see if this store had it.

When I got to the New Age area, I discovered three other very tall people there, two men and a woman, all about 35 years of age, and all with compelling, intense eyes gazing at me and each other. We all met in a cluster, standing close together. There was a feeling of electricity in the air and my ears were ringing as we all felt compelled to talk to each other at once. We were all buying the same book - *Star People*.

We had tears in our eyes, we were so happy to have discovered each other. The power in that room was amazing. As we stood together in happiness and recognition, it was like a reunion of souls, and there was a huge surge of electrical energy between us. I could see the energies around us were swirling and sparkling in gold and yellows. It was like we could reach each other's minds and did not need to talk. We all seemed tuned in to the same frequency.

I have met people whom I believe I knew from past lives but I have never had such an intense, powerful, and instant recognition along with a feeling of pure love as I did that day. It was as if we all knew this was a very fragile moment and did not have much time to talk, so there was an urgency to speak to each other quickly. We started to tell each other what we were doing in life. One of them was painting angels, another was working with mentally ill people, another was creating ceramic statues for healing and I told them someday I was going to write a book and address the subject of Star People.

We all nodded at each other in joyful appreciation of each other's lives and then we dispersed and melted into the crowd, all of us scattering in different directions. Although I still remember this odd moment with great clarity, even now twenty years later I marvel at what happened that day.

Star People

Jeannie is a dear young friend, yet an old, old soul.
I remember her from other places - something we both know.
In this, a huge, vast universe, there is a grand plan,
Even though we earthlings may not understand.

Jeannie explores other worlds, seeing other views,
It seems THIS is the foreign land, that we need to get through.

Our talks are most dynamic as we speak of many things.
What we feel in this huge cosmos may be really happening.

We both are spiritual warriors, fighting the good cause.
As Light Beings, and pioneers, this cause must not be lost.
There is so much in this world that humans do not know,
Yet one feels it with an intuition, feels it in one's soul.

*   *   *   *

I have dreams and visions of life in other lands,
Even though they sometimes may be hard to understand.
I see other worlds, and ways, and with this I have to deal.
It's often very difficult to explain what I may feel.

Are we all just earthlings, or do we come from some other star?
Do you ever yearn for worlds, in the universe afar?
I feel earth can be strange to me, not the other places.
I believe that many of us have extraterrestrial traces.

Star People in this galaxy may see other things,
It is not just imagination, but a truth which truly rings.
Stay open to these other lands - someday the world may see,
What humans do not understand will no longer be a mystery.

Eric's alien

The Chartreuse Green Streak

In Sedona, Arizona, there are places of high energy.
There are vortexes to visit, and amazing sights to see.
The red rocks remind me of other places, like energies of Egypt.
Sedona is a healing place, one I will not forget.
While staying at a motel atop a hill on that first night,
A very odd occurrence happened in the evening light.

The sun was setting in the west, yet it was warm and beautiful.
Later, underneath the moon, the night seemed very magical.
We were seated on the balcony which overlooked the town.
I was struck by the beauty of jutting red rocks, as I gazed around.
We had talked about the other worlds, and what we did believe.
We all were very open about what one could perceive.

When all of a sudden, in my view, a comet streaked across the sky.
Moving slowly and deliberately, it was easily seen with the naked eye.
Much bigger than a falling star, what could this green streak really be?
These two others viewed the same thing I did, as they sat with me.
This object swept into Boynton Canyon - that is how it looked to us.
But what was it, this strange colored light? - together we discussed.

We went there the next morning,
and found Boynton Canyon all blocked off,
They said the Air Force was doing testing -
but at this explanation we all scoffed.
I know it was something different, and not any kind of airplane.
I also felt that never ever would it be explained.
Intuitively, I knew that we had witnessed a phenomenon.
I am so glad we saw it, though it was strange and uncommon.

Life is very odd sometimes - to be in the right place and at the right time.
I am so glad we witnessed this, and felt it was a sign.
As an intuitive person, people talk to me a lot.
I often hear strange stories, as people tell me of their thoughts.
And I have found throughout the years, many odd things happen.
Much in life is mysterious, and sometimes we do tap in.

Galactic Dream

I dreamed of three ET's on Easter one year,
That although very shy, and though with their own fears,
These extraterrestrials stood at our door,
Making three booming knocks which I couldn't ignore.
Not knowing their strength, they knocked three times again,
Yet three more frightening knocks, though I felt they were friends.

I just knew that the callers were here to see me,
Yet at five in the morning, just who could it be?
I astral traveled through the door and out onto the steps,
And shyly they stood there - I will never forget.
I shook as I stood and leaned back on the door,
But with looks of compassion their eyes did implore.

They all stood there around me with high energies,
And the moment was charged with such electricity.
They were taller than me, with their movements quite slow.
Their whole bodies seemed fluid and looked like they glowed,
With eyes very huge - luminous, and quite bright,
I could not stop shaking, they caused such a fright.

They each held a present, as they stood around.
I accepted the gifts as they gazed shyly down.
Though I knew they were space creatures sent from above,
Yet I still felt surrounded with absolute love.
I was really quite shaken - time seemed to stand still.
Yet they loved me, I felt, and my heart was so filled.

These gift boxes were empty, but their message was real,
What really did matter was how they made me feel.
For these gifts represented - Faith, Hope, and Love.
And their message was meant for earth, sent from above.
Their eyes told me volumes as we all stood there,
I invited them in, and yet I was aware.

This moment was fragile - they really couldn't stay.
Yet we all had connected I felt on that day.
And poof, they were gone - my ears rang in my head.
I felt spaced out, and then I flipped back in my bed.
To me Easter is cosmic - there is much we don't know,
There are other worlds too, which reach out to our souls.

14
Spiritual Adventures in San Francisco

Pierre's Philosophy

When my pet mom came home from a trip to San Francisco, she was anxious to tell me about the adventures she'd had with animals. She knows I love to hear about other creatures in the world. She told me that during her visit to San Francisco she had visited the Grace Cathedral, which has an indoor as well as an outdoor labyrinth. A labyrinth is a walking prayer path that is shaped in a weaving pattern, encompassed by a circle. It is a spiritual tool for working with Spirit and to help people get in touch with their inner wisdom. To follow a labyrinth is to physically and spiritually perform a walking meditation or prayer.

This path was laid out on cement with lines in a pattern that flowed back and forth, ending in the middle of the labyrinth circle. My pet mom walked the labyrinth several times. The first day she was alone on the path except for five pigeons she discovered right in front of her when she reached the center of the circle. My pet mom said her prayer in the middle of the labyrinth and received her answer from Spirit. She then left the center, retracing the path out of the labyrinth.

Slowly, she walked out of the labyrinth and when she reached the end, she turned back to gaze at the circle. She thanked Spirit for her answer and right at that moment the five pigeons flew up from the center of the circle where they had remained the whole time.

I think I have my own labyrinth here at the house. The staircase runs one way down to the landing and then turns and runs the other way down to the bottom level. This may not seem like much to other members of this household but they are a lot of stairs for me, and it seems like a kind of animal labyrinth to me. My pet mom told me labyrinths are to go back and forth in different directions in order to help humans use both sides of their brains. All I know is that I like going up and down these stairs because it is great exercise, although I have been climbing them much more slowly in recent years.

The Grace Cathedral Labyrinth

Solitary Adventures

One evening during her San Francisco trip, my pet mom sat at the park in front of the Grace Cathedral, missing me. Many people would arrive at the park at that time of day with their dogs on leashes, then release them and let them have a run in the park. It was a time for the pet people and their dogs to socialize, all with their own pecking order of relationships.

In what seemed like a parade of dogs, the various animals of all sizes trotted around with their pet parents. Most of the dogs were on colorful leashes and some of the dogs wore jackets or even sweaters since it was a cool night. They would urinate and then race around each other. Sometimes they would tangle up their leashes or cords. It was quite the social hour.

Then on the way back to her daughter's apartment, my pet mom met an elderly lady who was feeding feral cats in the area. This lady had neutered and spayed eight cats in the neighborhood and then let them run in the backyard of a friend. This yard had a lot of weeds but also a shelter another friend had built out of wood, which was lined with old rugs. The kind lady fed the cats every day and said even though it was difficult to get close to them, she felt she was doing something for the cats of the world.

Another day, my pet mom walked down to the pier and watched two sea lions down by the docks, frolicking in the water. These seals were very expressive, making honking, harping noises for food.

Everywhere my pet mom travels, she looks for the animals and creatures to find her bliss.

Karla's Celestial Thoughts

Green Cathedral

Fern Canyon, California has a large gully or stream which runs down a mountain into the ocean. There are beautiful, lush green ferns everywhere. One afternoon, I hiked up this gully with my daughter and her friends and then back down again. It was a mysterious, moss covered stream we viewed as we hopped from rock to rock and it reminded me of a lush green cathedral of nature. It was serene and still except for this quiet stream of water running down the canyon, and so peaceful - God's own natural cathedral!

Muir Woods, Majestic Beings

The first time I saw the redwoods was near San Francisco when I went to Muir Woods, an enchanted forest. These majestic, wise old trees make you want to speak in hushed tones as they may overhear you, and you feel compelled to give them their due respect. Years later I was

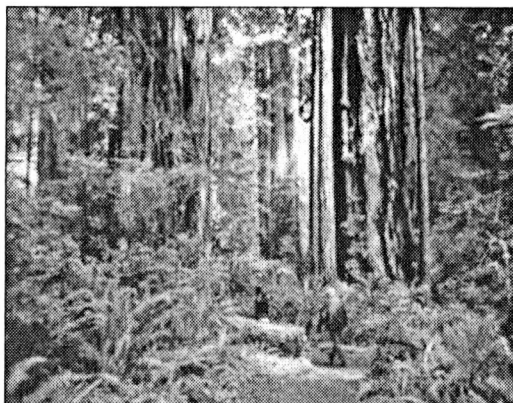

Majestic Redwoods

up at Humboldt University and saw bigger, more dramatic redwoods, appearing so mysterious in the mist, lovely and inspiring, seeming to reach up to the sky forever. I believe they teach us to be patient in life and to respect the power of nature. They are the elders of the trees.

Trinidad, California – Symphony by the Sea

I bravely try to listen to what nature has to say,
In the mystery of the ocean, awesome music seems to play.
I feel the rhythm of the sea while strolling by the ocean,
I love the peaceful energies, as they stir my emotions.

Some storms bring harsher melodies as their compositions play,
But if we listen carefully we gather truths from what they say.
Each day can be a serenade of golden lyrics, precious hours,
If we can just appreciate the joyful notes within our power.

Nature stirs a song of beauty deep within your heart,
You discover in the universe, you too have your own part.
As surely there are reasons why we each are here on earth,
With our own gifts and energies, and each with our own worth.

And so we each add something although sometimes it seems small.
Our goodness will shine through us, if we will accept our call.
There's a symphony of harmony in the ocean's many songs,
May you feel this harmony and hear the music, all year long!

Symphony by the sea

My Own Labyrinth

When I came home from this last trip to California, I created a labyrinth of my own in the woods near my home using rocks I collected from Lake Superior. I also bought a small hand labyrinth which has grooves filled with sand that can be traced with a finger. Any kind of labyrinth can be a useful tool. We can clarify a problem or ask for a solution. Labyrinths can help heal or release problems or help us feel rejuvenated and connected to Spirit. Every time I travel to California, I discover new cosmic tools for spirituality.

15
Dashing Dolphins of Maui

Pierre's Philosophy

After a few days in San Francisco, my pet mom and Hazel flew to Hawaii for ten days. I don't like to complain, but I really missed my pet mom. She did explain everything she was going to do before she left me, and Caroline and my pet dad remained here in Minnesota with me, but it was not the same. The first week I was okay but the second week was intolerable. I am accustomed to my pet mom petting me, grooming me with a comb and giving me extra tuna treats.

Mystical Hawaii

So I was elated when she returned from her trip, although it was two days later than she had originally anticipated. I was aloof towards her for about half an hour when she came back home but then I could not stand it anymore. I love her too much, and finally threw my paws around her neck as usual. The second night she was home, my pet mom held me in her arms and told me this magical story about Maui.

Karla's Celestial Thoughts

Ever since I saw dolphins performing at Sea World in Florida when I was young, I was on a quest to see them in the sea. I wished to see them in their own habitat, doing their own thing. I believe dolphins represent deep communication in life and profound openings to psychic awareness.

At 6:00 in the morning one day on Maui, Hazel and I drove to the south end of the island along the coast, with the silky sun of Hawaii rising. Dew sparkled on the gorgeous multicolored array of flowers along the side of the road. My daughter and I felt like we were truly in a paradise on earth. We stopped at the end of the road where black lava reefs lined the seashore.

We met the sea captain, Paul, who owned his own sea kayak business, and he suited us up for a trip out to sea, hopefully to view dolphins and to go snorkeling. On this morning the sea was calm and beautiful and I thought a kayak adventure would be so much fun and so easy. Boy, was I wrong! Sometimes it is good if we don't know how difficult adventures may be in our lives. That way we are well into them before we can possibly change our minds!

Sometimes the lessons we need to learn surprise us.

A Gift from the Dolphins

Our group followed Paul's kayak after he launched our kayaks off the reefs. After about 20 minutes of paddling, we were instructed by the captain to stop and hook our kayaks together in a long row, front to back. Paul informed us that the dolphins had been sighted in the distance and were coming in from the sea. This was one of the places they visited frequently.

Our group put on snorkeling gear and fins and were shown how to smoothly roll off the kayaks into water, which was about 25 feet deep. We relaxed in the waves, waiting for the dolphins. My daughter and I were wearing life preservers, bobbing up and down in the waves anticipating, when suddenly - there they were! About 20 dolphins came weaving through all of the people in the water, full of joy and exuberance. The dolphins were sociable, unafraid and amazingly tame as they intermingled with us. They seemed happy to play and socialize with humans. Swirling around with high healing energies, and seemingly smiling faces, these friendly creatures were like angels of the sea.

They all rushed up to the surface, jumping up and then diving down into the depths of the sea again all together. Like a giant black and white rainbow arc, they wove their way around the group of humans floating in the water. Energies of healing and communication seemed to emanate from them. The dolphins electrified the aqua waters of the South Seas.

After a half-hour of this magical time with the dolphins, we pulled ourselves back up onto our kayaks and unhooked them from each other. We followed the captain's kayak again as we paddled further along the shore line. Paul led us to shore, keeping his own kayak on the inside of our line near the jagged lava reefs. When we reached shore we parked our boats and snorkeled in the shallows of a large pool of lava reefs. There we viewed many kinds of fish - bright yellow and blue, a strange purple fish, an eel and other sea creatures.

I was so impressed by this whole world of nature, where there was such a tranquil, calm beauty to be found. It was another world - a place of quiet wonder. Like finding heaven under the sea.

Overcoming Adversity

Finally, it was time to paddle back to shore to the original site where the kayaks had been launched. Meanwhile, a huge wind had come up on the sea making it difficult to return. The captain instructed us to hook all our kayaks back together as we attempted to paddle in unison.

Because of the increasing wind, swirling waves were growing bigger in the sea. One of the kayaks tipped over but the captain turned it upright again. A person in one of the other kayaks became sick but everyone had to keep going anyway. With focus, teamwork and a lot of paddling, we all made it back to shore where we were complimented by the captain. I felt especially proud of myself as I was the oldest in the group. It was quite an adventure, like a survival trip, and Pierre seemed to purr with pride as I shared my story with him.

A Visit from the Giant Sonar Fish

Years ago, my husband Joe and I went shelling on Sanibel Island in the middle of the day at low tide - the best time for shelling. We were wading in the water almost up to our hips with a space of about 20 feet between us. All of a sudden a powerful huge force came roaring in between us, gracefully sweeping up small fish in its mouth and quickly but smoothly turning around and racing out to sea again.

It happened so fast we were both standing there frozen and unmoving as we tried to gather our wits. A dolphin had sped by us, a small magnetic force in the water, and yet it went by so quietly, barely causing a ripple. It left us with a great sense of awe. This was one single dolphin but it emanated such a joyful energy as it sliced through the water with its raw silver strength, truly a master of the sea.

Each leaf, flower, snowflake, raindrop or wave in the sea is different from another, and a mystery. An experience with nature can awaken us to the power of these forces. Be adventurous in life, and try new things!

Triumph by the sea

16
Animal & People Heaven

Pierre's Philosophy

It was difficult when Dozer died, but he was very old and it was a natural thing. He made the transition quickly. My pet mom told me she had talked to Casper a few days before he died while they were sitting outside on the front lawn. She thanked him for being such a wonderful pet. He had indeed been a terrific dog. She

Pierre Dreaming

sat and held him with her arms wrapped around his neck as tears rolled down her cheeks. He had a smile on his face, as usual.

Then there was Streak, the first dog my pet mom took care of without Joe's help. She had never had a dog of her own before. When he was about eight years old, Streak died suddenly in a car accident. The truth was that he had almost been killed several times before. He never was "street smart," and often was not paying attention. He had been living on borrowed time for quite a while.

Sometimes it is harder to lose pets unexpectedly than it is to have the time to say good-bye to them when they are ill. The week when I got really sick, my pet mom was crying a lot and adjusting to the fact that I might die. This has helped her to prepare for my eventual death.

She was told I have cataracts, arthritis, and some kidney and liver problems. I am losing some patches of fur on the back of my haunches but I am still hanging in there. Sometimes losing a pet can be much more devastating than losing a human. Unlike humans, we always love unconditionally. Humans can be totally vulnerable with us, honest and caring. We have no hidden agenda. Therefore, we are easier to love but that can also make it harder to let go.

When Streak died, my pet mom was understandably upset for a few weeks, and still misses him sometimes. It is hard to get over a death but one can adjust after a while, remembering the good memories without so much pain.

More Than a Dream

One night about three weeks after Streak died, my pet mom dreamed about him. At this point, Casper had been dead for a few years and Dozer had died long before. In the dream, she went outside to sit on the front steps and was putting on her shoes to go walking. It was a beautiful spring day. All of a sudden, along came Streak, Casper and Dozer, all three of them together, rushing up to the steps.

Streak charged into my pet mom. He licked her hands as he always did and grinned up at her as only he could do. He had an unearthly glow about him and looked younger - all three of the dogs did, and as my pet mom greeted them with joy, she knew this was more than just a dream.

She thanked them all for coming and for having been with her for a while in this life. Streak looked up at her with a knowing gaze and then went off with his friends racing around in a pack. What a wonderful way to have a doggie heaven in another dimension. This was a most comforting dream for my pet mom. She felt it was a real dimension - an animal heaven. Our spirits live forever!

Sometimes you may feel we are around you after we die. You may think you are dreaming about us when we are really visiting you in

Spirit. We may bring you messages in many ways from the other side. This is a wonderful expression of our love for you.

Karla's Celestial Thoughts

The Accident

Animals have forgiving hearts. One of my friends accidentally ran over her pet cat with a car. She was exceedingly upset about this and could not forgive herself for a long time. I believe her cat forgave her and understood. I think sometimes animals have a contract to be on earth for a certain time and no matter what happens, they are going to go up to the spirit world when it is time for them to leave earth. I believe they are forgiving and have universal love and compassion in their hearts. They understand.

Sometimes there is a merciful step to destiny, as when we need to put a pet to sleep. Their quality of life is no longer viable and it is time. Our pets are accepting and much wiser than humans. Pierre astral traveled to me as a kitten, proving to me that he had a soul. Pets often will come again in a dream or a feeling or some event, to show they are still around us. Our dear ones are never truly gone.

Miracles come with transitional experiences. I know someone who had the painful situation of putting her 21 year old Rag Doll cat to sleep. Her son came home from the Air Force the day before this happened and she felt her cat had understood and waited to say good-bye to her son before passing away. The woman thanked her cat for hanging on until then.

We had a similar experience. We made an appointment to bring Casper to the vet to be put to sleep as he was in pain and very ill, but he died on his own an hour before the appointment.

Merciful Help to Destiny

Sometimes in life, though difficult, you have to put your pet to sleep.
You struggle and you agonize, but relief is what they seek.
There are many reasons why this sometimes must be done,
But pets are family members, and you may feel quite undone.

My sister's cat was very ill - "Me Too" was her name.
It was so hard; this beloved pet was in a lot of pain.
I helped her as I brought her cat into the city vet.
And it was hard for me as well, with my own pangs of regret.

Driving through a winter snowstorm in the freezing cold,
I helped her with her pet who was so weak, so sick, so old.
I let my guilty feelings go, as her time had come,
Although it was quite agonizing, I knew it must be done.

At the vets, she was so restless; I held her and she settled down.
I was glad that I could comfort her and so I stayed around.
She gazed at me with her wise eyes and I felt that she knew.
It was her time - she seemed to tell me, something we must do.

She accepted her own fate, which made it easier for me.
Then it was over, as she was released from pain and agony.
I know there is a special place where animals find peace.
I am comforted they have a heaven, where they all find release.

I know that pets do understand; our two hearts are together.
We never really lose them; they are in our hearts forever.
Although we miss our little friends who have value we can't measure,
We will be with them, in heaven someday -
these, our cherished treasures.

Bowing Out Gracefully

I hope someday it will be legal to help people die if they are going through difficult transitions and are ready to pass on. I have told people in readings that they may sometimes need to let a relative or loved one know that it is all right for them to die, that this person is waiting for permission in order to let go. Sometimes souls hang on for someone in the family when they really want to make the transition to the other side. It is selfish of us to try to keep them here when it is their time to go.

My mother was in hospice in the hospital, and at one point we needed to make the decision to let her go and quit feeding her intravenously. Give people the opportunity to die with respect and to have the spiritually uplifting experience of being in control of their own destinies.

Dad's Final Gift

My dad, Hans, died of a heart attack in the middle of the night, out at my parent's lake cottage. The next morning when my siblings and I arrived together at the cottage, all of us were upset and stunned. It was so sudden; all we could do was try our best to cope with the devastating news. We were in the kitchen conversing when a delivery man arrived with a dozen red roses. Were they from someone who had already heard the news about our dad?

The man handed my mom some beautiful, fragrant red roses, with a card attached that read, "From Hans". As instructed by Dad, his secretary had ordered the roses to be sent on this day. He passed away on their wedding anniversary July 9th, and those roses were his final gift to his bride.

Spirit in the Fishing Gear

Two weeks later I was not coping very well with my dad's death. He was only 63 and it had been so sudden. I awakened on this morning and half opened my eyes, startled to see a vision of a white being standing in the threshold of our bedroom doorway. My dad stood in his old fishing gear with a soft smile on his face. I knew in a flash he had come to tell me he was okay, and everything was fine. And then I felt peace wash over me, along with acceptance and gratitude.

The Premonition

Many years ago I dreamed of Mom curled up in a fetal position, appearing light like a ghost or spirit. The next morning I drove to her house to take her to a doctor's appointment but she didn't answer my knock so I unlocked the door and let myself in. I found her in the bedroom sleeping curled up, just like the vision. Once again, a feeling of peace and acceptance washed over me and I knew our mother was going to die soon. It was a premonition. I tiptoed into her bathroom alone, and cried. Then I pulled myself together and faced the future.

Celestial Tunnel

When my mother was dying of cancer I visited her every day for the last three weeks of her life. Sitting by her bedside, I felt free to tell her many of my thoughts as I processed the many different emotions I was going through. All of a sudden she awakened and became animated. She talked of seeing a long tunnel going towards a light and told me that God was preparing a place for her, her own room. The moment was poignant and beautiful.

My mother was a complicated woman with some shadows in her life but was also a valiant, indomitable, courageous and brave spirit. I am glad she was my mother in this life.

Christmas Miracle

On that last Christmas Eve with my mother, she was in a coma. A neurologist told us she was brain dead and did not know what was going on but I quickly informed him that was nonsense. It turned out I was right!

I had driven back home to have a Christmas dinner with my family and then came back to the hospital to be with my mom. When I arrived at the hospital that night, Mother awakened out of her coma. She looked right at me and squeezed my hand. I was overjoyed to find her awake and alert, and quickly called my siblings to come down and be with us at the hospital. We all sat by her bed, talking to her on this final Christmas Eve together. Before she had gone into a coma, she had had a tracheotomy operation because of cancer of the throat and could not talk. She batted her eyes once for "yes," and twice for "no," and we laughed, cried and shared this magical time together, experiencing the true meaning of Christmas - Love!

Joe's Dream

As my mother's time of death drew near, I decided to stay right at the hospice with her. On New Year's Eve there were eight inches of snow and the road conditions were slippery, yet Joe asked if I wanted him to drive down to the hospital. He knew my mother was very close to death and thought I might need support, but I said that I could handle it alone. That's when he told me about a dream he'd had the night before.

Joe seldom remembers his dreams, so this was unusual. He dreamed my mother told him not to come down to the hospital to visit her because the weather was too bad. My intuitive reaction supported this, so perhaps a bad accident was even avoided. Joe said the dream seemed real - like she was truly there, which I'm sure she was. I think that when people are close to death they astral travel a lot and their spirit is in and out of their bodies. I believe Mom came to Joe in Spirit that night and it was somehow very comforting.

New Year's Day Miracle

Mom wanted to die in 1981 instead of 1980 for tax purposes, something none of us cared about, but she did. We realized what she was trying to do, so even though she had lapsed back into her coma by this time, we reminded her of what time it was on New Year's Eve. When we told her she made it to the New Year, she let out a huge sigh.

Sometimes certain times or numbers have significance to a person. The time 3:15 has always been important to me for many reasons, and I often notice special occurrences at this time. It was 3:15 a.m. when I had fallen asleep in a chair beside her bed, holding her hand. A nurse awakened me to tell me my mother had just died.

Mom made her goal. I also realized later she was waiting for me to go to sleep so she could make the transition into the next world alone. That was the way she lived her life, unselfishly. I am proud of her.

Tap on the Shoulder

A year after my father-in-law's death, my mother-in-law was sitting in their living room. All of a sudden she awakened quite startled. She said she felt her husband touch her shoulder and as she turned to talk to him, he whispered "Happy anniversary."

Three Men with AIDS

I know three men who died of AIDS - all of them so young and brave.
Why, oh why, were they all taken -
their young lives lost, their world forsaken?
There must be a cure for AIDS someday, for this I do fervently pray.
And meanwhile, God, do bless their souls -
these three young men, I loved them so.

The Suicide

We knew her such a little while, she briefly touched our lives.
And yet she made her mark much more than she would realize.
We all wanted to help her, but she was too hard to reach.
But every single star that falls has a lesson it may teach.

You never truly know people, deep inside their minds.
The tragedy is the difficulty of what depression finds.
She was a shooting star who streaked across our paths too fast.
No one could change her poor decision, so the die was cast.

She will never be forgotten,
Souls don't die in vain.
Every person is a gift,
And part of her remains.

I know there is a place for every human and creature in heaven and that people and animals who have crossed over continue to help us as angels from above. No soul is ever lost. Like the waves of the ocean that break and come onto shore, each wave represents a life when we are here on earth. We are alive for a while and then go back into the undertow, pulled into the ocean again. We are born into a new life, like a new wave coming in - breaking once more before we are pulled back into the sea. We live, we die, and we live again.

17
Angels all Around

Pierre's Philosophy

Through the Looking Glass

I have been in some dangerous situations over the years wherein I do believe I got some extra help from Spirit. One of these times my pet mom and dad were both at work. No one was home with me and a summer storm had swept in across the lake. My pet mom had forgotten to close the windows as it was a clear day and she didn't know a storm was coming. Sometimes storms in Minnesota can be very lively, and this one seemed to be so, with green hues in its clouds. It was quite eerie looking outside.

I am a very calm cat and don't usually get excited about storms but this one was different. I was sitting in the living room eyeing the storm when a northwest wind blew so fiercely it actually blew out a screen from the open window. I had never seen this before and I slowly and cautiously walked up to gaze out the window.

Now, the natural curiosity of a cat can be a dangerous thing. I knew I should not go through the open window and yet it was so tempting. Even though the wind and rain were sprinkling water on my whiskers, I stood on the window ledge staring into the tempest of the storm.

I was sniffing the air, thinking about the consequences of jumping out of the window onto the outside porch when I heard the key in the door. My pet mom bounded up the stairs two steps at a time, intuitively feeling the danger in the air. She found me in my precarious place and swept me up in her arms, holding me closely and whispering many endearing words of gratitude as I purred.

Actually, I was glad she made the decision for me and I did not have to deal with the danger. I am not sure I would have fared very well in the elements or that I would have ever gotten back through the window again. She kept muttering something about angels and God but I was just grateful to be getting extra special petting and love from her!

Fleas and More Fleas

I suspect Divine intervention was involved when Jamaica, the black and tan hound dog, visited us and someone sneaked her into the house for the night. Unfortunately, in a few days the fleas she left with us made their presence known. They were awful and my pet mom and I were both upset. Besides having to try to get them off of me with my long, long fur, she had to deal with washing about 20 loads of blankets, sheets, and shag rugs.

She was muttering to herself for a week about this tough situation and the flea dipping was terrible. Both my pet mom and dad had to hold me and dip me in the bathtub. They had to dip me three consecutive times in a week before all of the pesky critters would disappear. I really did not feel like fighting for my health at the time but I knew my pet mom still needed me in her life so I struggled and persevered. Again, she kept thanking angels and God.

Karla's Celestial Thoughts

Bright Tapestry

Angels weave a tapestry with golden threads of love.
I have often felt them with me, sent from heaven above.
The threads they weave are joyful with their patterns of bright cheer.
Without their intervention I feel I would not be here.

Sometimes life's storms or difficulties are blessings in disguise.
There is a plan for all of us we may not realize.

I have lived through miracles and am happy to be here.
I believe in angels - that they often are quite near.

They weave their golden threads to help us, though we're unaware.
These messengers of light and hope administer their care.
I have had unusual times and close calls I survived.
Because of these pure miracles, my faith has truly thrived.

I don't tune into negatives, but positives that have been.
Our lives are blessed with joy if we will trust our faith within.
I thank and honor angels - they assist me every day
I have abiding faith in them - they always show the way.

Close Calls in Childhood

I was born at home in a blizzard on March 3, 1941. The neighbors tried to shovel out several feet of snow so my mom could get to the hospital but it was impossible. Luckily, there was a doctor down the street who managed to make his way through the snow to our house in order to deliver me.

There is humor in some of the experiences I have had in my life as they are so outrageous! When I was two years old, I caused a lot of chaos in my family. One time I bounced right over my crib when I was supposed to be taking a nap and caught my head in between two spokes. I hung there upside-down, and fortunately my mother thought I was being too quiet and came to check on me. She discovered me turning blue, grabbed and held me and yelled for my older siblings to get help.

When I was five years old I got lost in our huge woods. My brother was supposed to be watching me but was playing with friends and got distracted. I liked to go out into nature but unfortunately this was winter and I was very grateful when a firefighter finally found me and brought me home. My mother dropped me into a warm bathtub, snowsuit and all, so I could thaw out.

One sunny afternoon when I was six years old, my sister and I walked to the neighborhood store where a man stopped his car and tried to entice us to get into his vehicle by offering us candy. I was tempted but my sister grabbed my hand before I could reach the door.

When she grabbed my hand she seemed to have an extra strength. We ran for our lives, all the way home. I shudder to think of what could have happened.

A couple of years later, when I was eight years old, one of my mother's friends was in charge of six of us kids and drove us out to Lake Calhoun in Minneapolis. I got in over my head and since I could not swim, I ended up going under. The lifeguard didn't see it happen but fortunately someone else discovered me when he happened to step on top of my body in the lake. They dragged me out just in the nick of time and resuscitated me. I remember having a flash of scenes from my life appear before my eyes, and seeing a bright light.

At 17 I crossed a street as a car sped around the curve, coming at me from out of nowhere. A voice told me to "jump up," and with faith that is what I did. Luckily this man had a running board on the side of his old car, which I somehow landed on, and I clung to the open window until he slowed down and stopped. Amazingly, I was unharmed. My dad, who was waiting for me at a nearby restaurant, was pale when I returned, saying he just knew something had happened. I had only crossed the street to get a newspaper so we could check out what movies were playing but Dad said he'd been very uneasy about me crossing that street. It was one of the few times he talked about using psychic abilities to get a sense of the future.

At 18 I just missed being struck by a train when the car I was in was almost hit, but I managed to get it off the train tracks just in time. On another occasion I went shopping with my kids when they were young and we ended up coming back from Minneapolis in an unexpected snowstorm. The brakes went out, but fortunately not until we reached home.

I had a close call once again when I was 35 and had to have an emergency operation. Although I was scheduled for surgery two days later, something was terribly wrong. I was cold and shaking, and Joe had to keep piling blankets on me to keep me warm. When we called the doctor he insisted I come to the hospital immediately. I found out later that I was slowly hemorrhaging and going into shock. They said it was a good thing I got to the hospital when I did because I would not have made it another day. Angels helped again.

Another close call happened when I was driving Caroline to Arcata, California where she was to attend school. I was about 40 at this time, enjoying our trip through the mountains. However, when we approached one of the curves, a logging truck appeared up ahead – and being in the wrong lane, it was headed right into us! I lurched a bit, the other driver did the same, and somehow we missed each other. We also missed the steep incline on our other side, which was, perhaps, even more amazing. This mountaintop was at an altitude of about 5000 feet and my heart was in my throat; it was so frightening. But somehow we made it around that corner safely!

Logging truck adventure

More Angelic Help

My eldest son, Forrest, and I were flying in a little puddle jumper airplane from Augusta to Atlanta, Georgia, in a rainstorm when I was 43. We had been on a trip to see relatives in Aiken, South Carolina. We were the last plane to come in that night, and the dials on the pilot's board were all lit up as we flew through the turbulent skies. The airport was such a welcome sight through the lightning, thunder, and rain. We made a three point landing that night.

When I was 44, I was robbed by a taxi cab driver while traveling in Mexico. My friends and I were okay and grateful to be alive, although we had to go through a big hassle after that, trying to get money wired to us. Somehow, we made it through, living on crackers and water for two days before finally being able to leave the country and get back to the United States.

On another trip when I was 44, in Glacier Park, Montana, I got caught up at the "Blind Pass," in a snowstorm. I had driven there alone and hiked by myself while my daughter was working. The weather report predicted sunny skies for the next few days but the report was wrong and conditions changed. I wound my way slowly down the mountain top, only able to see about five feet ahead of me, and trying to stay within the lines all the way down the mountain.

On a Minnesota freeway one stormy summer day, I was riding with my youngest son, Eric, who was driving. An electrical pole tore loose and cracked, landing by us on the ground. The pole sheared off the driver's mirror, hitting the driver's side, and yet the pole and lines missed our car on this wild, chaotic ride. The lightning lit the sky ablaze as we hydroplaned with no control for a long mile or two.

At 59, I became sick on Christmas Eve. Overnight, my left eye became completely swollen. It turned out I had cellulitis and was very ill, ending up in urgent care at our local hospital. I felt like I was "checking out." With medication the doctors were able to get this under control, however, and I was able to get back home.

I have felt the help of Spirit many, many times, and continually count my blessings.

Angel Threads on Ice

In December, with a major snowstorm I was driving through,
I had to get to work that day, but it was hard to do.
I was on a four-lane highway, driving cautiously.
The traffic grew quite heavy, it was building up by me.

A car appeared from nowhere, speeding down this busy road.
It skidded on the highway, and I knew the brakes wouldn't hold.
As this car sped into traffic, the driver tried to hit the brakes.
He did not pump them correctly, which was his big mistake.

So I prayed for help from angels, as we needed them right now,
And I felt they would assist us, though I didn't know quite how.
Although odds were stacked against us, not a single car was hit.
It seemed like validation to me - proof so definite.

His vehicle wove through traffic, missing every car that day,
In a most amazing feat and good maneuvering display.
Another time, another place, where angels were right there,
Helping people, although it's true, we might not be aware.

Many People Have Close Calls

Although many people have close calls, mine helped me appreciate,
Life is so very fragile, as these stories seem to demonstrate.
Many people have tough times and big storms in their lives.
My little stories just helped me know, they helped me realize.

Life is a precious gift, we often take for granted.
Because I sometimes had close calls, my views may be quite slanted.
But I think we should awaken to the value of this life,
And always see the positive - keep good things in our sights.

Many people have dark struggles, harder times they will go through,
And sometimes deep dilemmas when they don't know what to do.
There are wars, and murders, near deaths,
tough things happening each day,
But that is when we find our answers if we stop and pray.

Some people live with cancer - each day they bravely fight.
Others - heart disease or strokes - they fight this in their lives.
Addictions can be terrible, sad things happen every day.
These storms can be horrendous, on the people they may prey.

I know there is a dark side with some deeper, darker horrors.
I know that in reality they should not be ignored.
Though life has many dangers, I still believe in God.
I still have faith and hope, and know He is my lightning rod.

I believe through everything, God will always care,
Even though we may not feel Him or are not aware.
I do believe through everything, angels are here too.
Even though it may not seem like they are helping you.

I feel the joy of being alive; more people should each day.
No matter what their problems are, or what may come their way.
Life is a Celestial Garden, where our lives may flourish.
We each have sacred spiritual ground where our souls are nourished.

We each create our garden where we may expand and grow.
If we listen to our many lessons, we expand our souls.
Angels spin their webs with thread and help us every day.
So I thank and honor all of them for showing us the way.

Angels are mysterious light beings. I believe they can appear as humans or in animal form, or in other unexpected forms. They may be large or small, apparent at times, or hidden. I believe Pierre has been an angel cat all along. It took me quite a while to realize what should have been obvious from the beginning. But God has His timing.

Angels may be simply unexplainable but what matters is that we begin to believe and understand, and be open to the possibility that we may be receiving Divine help, especially if or when we ask for it. The more we ask for help, the more help we receive.

18
Faith and Renewal

Pierre's Philosophy

We all have opportunities to grow and to help each other while we are here on earth. Always give animals a chance and realize there are reasons to have pets, and that these reasons will be revealed as you go along the joyful journey of life. Sometimes we are reincarnated several times with you because our life spans are shorter than yours. We have a job to perform with you and we keep coming back until you get our message. I feel we are here to do as much good and to spread as much joy as we can while on earth.

Karla's Celestial Thoughts

Angels Again

Since my mother's death years ago, I often have some kind of contact from her on the day of her birthday. On my mother's birthday in September, Hazel and I drove to Wisconsin to visit one of my Seven Sister friends and then continued on up to Door County peninsula overnight. On this trip we drove for miles exploring the whole island.

When we left Door County, we stopped at a large garden shop to view many lawn ornaments, and as we were leaving the store I expressed an interest in a gargoyle statue which I liked. It reminded me of our trip, and of Hazel's love of Paris, and I regretted not buying it because I love finding unusual statues for my gardens back home.

The next day we drove again on many rural roads, often seeing very little traffic in our explorations, returning to our town in Minnesota late at night. We were within the last ten miles of our trip when all of a sudden we felt a huge jerk with the car like the car was not quite in gear, and the pedal did not seem to be getting any gas but we pushed to keep going as we were by now very close to home. Fortunately, there was no traffic on this stretch of the road and we managed to hurry through two stop signs, get up the last hill, and then coast down it before reaching the old dirt road which turns into our driveway.

We glided jerkily down the road, rounded the corner and slid to a stop in our parking area when suddenly smoke started streaming out of the hood and billowing up to the sky. So, after hours and hours of driving we were able to successfully return home before the car broke down. The next day we learned that the transmission had gone out in our car. I believe the spirit of my mother was helping us on that journey.

The following day, a friend came into my workplace with a gargoyle statue she had found, saying she knew it was meant for me. This woman runs a pet-care business and had been in a hurry after leaving a client's house when she backed into a dumpster that tipped over sideways, causing this statue to roll out onto the ground.

This woman, who also works at a metaphysical store, talks to angels as an everyday experience. She said the angels told her to bring this to me! When I asked her which day it was that all this happened, I discovered she had found the gargoyle on my mother's

a Gargoyle at Notre Dame in Paris

birthday. She had definitely tuned into my wishes and I believe my own special angel, my mother, must have been communicating with me from the other side.

An Angel Pin

I recently had an intuitive reading with a client and kept feeling many angels around her. That day when I left the store where I do readings, I could not get this woman out of my mind. I happened to have a happy face angel pin in my purse and decided I had to give it to her. I felt so compelled to give it to her immediately that I had to find her.

She worked in the same town I work in so I drove to her workplace and parked my car. I walked across the street to her store and right then she happened to be driving by, as she had forgotten some item in town that she needed. Timing can be quite phenomenal. It turned out that it was not her day to work but she needed something in a store that just happened to be on the road I was on.

She was stopped at the traffic light and I hurried to catch her attention.

"I don't know why you need this," I said, handing her the pin through her car window, "but I felt like you needed some extra help right now."

She looked startled to see me and a little bit confused, but I was greatly relieved after the angel pin was safely in her hands.

Weeks later she called my workplace to tell me what had happened. Two hours after I gave her this angel pin she found out her mother had been airlifted to a hospital over in Wisconsin due to a heart attack. This woman's next three weeks were extremely hectic as she tried to deal with everything involving her mother. She told me one of the things that got her through all of it was knowing that angels are real, and that they were helping. Her mother did die, but even that was easier since this experience helped to both support and prepare her for what she had to face. She was able to accept the fact that it was her mother's time to pass on.

Angel Cat

I think my own angel cat, Pierre, has been here to help me become much more aware of the Divine assistance which is in my life constantly. He makes me realize angels are everywhere, helping us all the time. Ever since he entered my life, I have awakened to the importance of animals, and also angels.

The Smile

She slipped quickly through the entrance, her tail waving a hello.
This new grand dog broke all house rules,
but one simply couldn't say "no."
She hopped up on our sofa with a pure angelic charm,
Willow visited just overnight, but we were quite disarmed.

For, the corners of her mouth curled and transformed into a smile,
We could not ignore her energies - she exuded grace and style.
Then the smile became a huge grin of pure happiness and glee.
She had conquered us with love, and proved she TOO is "family."

Eric and Jamaica

Caroline and Jamaica

Forrest and Willow

Hazel and Pierre

19
There's a Poodle in the Swamp

Pierre's Philosophy

On a hot, humid day in July, my pet mom and her daughter Hazel were visiting out on the balcony overlooking the lake. It was early morning, the sun was already hot and the birds were singing. It was a wonderful day. Suddenly two cars drove down the road, quickly stopping in the parking lot, and two couples emerged from their cars. They did not pay any attention to the ladies on the balcony, but instead were intently focused on the woods by the house.

My pet mom descended from the steps and hurried up to the people. One of the men told her they were looking for a miniature white poodle that had just crossed the busy highway and then ran down the road, disappearing into the woods. They said it appeared frightened and confused and had nearly been hit by a car.

These two couples were in a hurry so my pet mom told them she would continue to look for the dog and thanked them for caring enough to stop. After getting a leash and piece of bread to entice the dog, she carefully searched the trails in the woods. Although she looked and looked, the lost poodle was nowhere to be found so my pet mom returned to the house. About a half hour later, she and Hazel were sitting on the balcony again discussing where to look next when they heard a loud barking coming from the swamp near the woods. My pet mom sighed, knowing how difficult it would be to get this dog out of the swamp, but she put on some old clothes and boots and tramped out into the muck.

The cattails and weeds were thick and high, towering over her head. My pet mom used her arms to cut a swath through the woods, following the high barking voice. Finally, she reached the lost dog. He was a frightened little poodle, weighing scarcely over ten pounds, with darkened muddy feet and belly. The poor creature looked like a lost little lamb and was wearily going in circles, appearing disoriented and upset.

My pet mom realized the dog was too upset to approach when it snapped at her from fear and began shaking. She quickly sat down in the mud and dirt, getting down to the level of the poodle. Then, my pet mom patiently called to the dog and waited for it to approach her and smell the outstretched hands that she held low so as not to intimidate the creature. She offered a piece of bread as gently as possible. The poodle finally approached her and crawled into her arms, shaking like a leaf.

The dog ignored the food; it only wanted comfort. Stroking the dog and calmly reassuring it, she got it to calm down and with the poodle on one arm, slowly wound her way through the swamp land. My pet mom carefully watched her footing, going from clump to clump, using her free hand to push the large cattails once more to the side. Finally, she reached the road and emerged with the dog.

Hazel and my pet mom fed the dog, put it on a leash and made a bed by the steps out of an old box and blanket. They called neighbors, made flyers on the computer and drove around asking people if they knew anyone who had lost a dog. Later that evening they were able to locate the owners and reunite the dog with its pet mom. They found out someone in the family had been negligent about letting the dog out and had not paid attention to the fact it needed to be watched more closely.

This dog was 13 years old and almost completely blind and deaf. It was a total miracle the dog could be saved that day. This was a real lesson to the people in the family, that they had to pay more attention to the needs of this elderly dog. Unfortunately, many people are sometimes unaware of the needs of a pet, particularly an older pet.

Be aware of us, as pets. We are valuable, too. Pay attention to our needs, please. We love you unconditionally. Please love us back.

Karla's Celestial Thoughts

I often have "Poopsie alerts" for Pierre, where I check every few hours to be sure he has not gotten into some closet or other kind of potential trouble. Our pets are members of the family, after all. It was when I prayed for the poodle and hoped I could find it soon that I was able to determine exactly where it was. In spite of the swampland, I made a beeline towards the voice and discovered the spot where the dog was hidden. He wanted help and yet was hiding from me as I called to him. He was afraid to be discovered. Finding out later that he was blind and deaf made me realize just how scary all of this must have been for him at the time.

Pets and Nature

There is a magic in this world, Pierre helps me to see.
A place of grace, a place of hope, a place of majesty.
With his love, unconditional, he makes me so aware.
We can improve the universe if we will only care.

Animals show us a design - in our lives they play a part.
They thread their way into our lives and live within our hearts.
Together we create a world, and tapestry of care,
As our pets may awaken us, and make us more aware.

Pets are a special joy in the living they convey.
They live life every moment, and appreciate each golden day.
The beauty that you see in nature, painted strokes of artistry,
Can also be a source of joy and so fulfill a need.

The awesome mountains, scented pine trees, lone cry of a loon,
Bright sunsets, sparkling lights on lakes created by the moon.
The painted desert and Grand Canyon - ever changing shades,
A blooming cactus in the desert, fragile beauty made.

Palm trees swaying in the breeze, seagulls flying high.
Shelling treasures in the sand as sandpipers scoot by.
A delicate soft snowflake, or a bird's sweet melody
So many patterns formed in nature seem quite heavenly.

When nature seems too quiet, listen - you may start to hear.
With courage of convictions you will conquer any fears.
Be brave and pay attention to what nature says each day.
Even in the deepest silence strong music will play.

In stillness, you may hear a song from deep within your heart,
And discover in the universe you too have your own part.
As surely there are reasons why we all are here on earth,
Each of us with gifts to bring and each with our own worth.

And so we do add something, though it sometimes may seem small.
Our goodness will shine through us, if we will accept our call.
There's a symphony of harmony in seasons of these songs.
May you simply hear the melody and music all year long.

So let us feel the magic in this world so full of grace.
As animals may help us see, the world's an awesome place.
May we feel the wondrous power of God - it should not be ignored,
And messages of nature should forever be explored.

Awesome Mountains

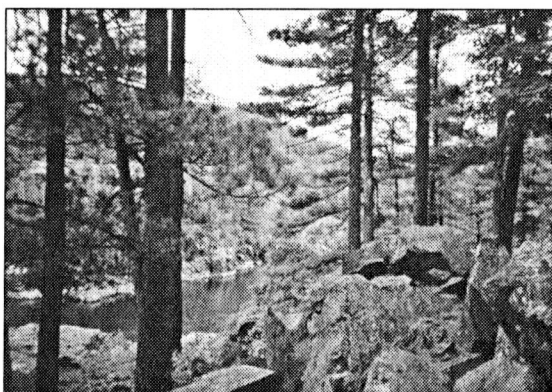

Scented Pine Trees

Grand Canyon

Strong Music Playing

Palm trees swaying in the breeze

This angelic pet time story was truly influenced by Pierre. He brought Divine vibrations to this book and has helped me to realize that this book, my cards and my ideas about animals should be brought out to the world so people begin to realize that animals do bring messages to the world every single day. Pierre has shared so many celestial thoughts throughout the years as I hold him and he purrs. He is my angel cat!

Epilogue

As I dictate this to my pet mom, I am still here helping in any way I can. She told me someday she would save my ashes after I die and have a ceremony, spreading my ashes in the woods. I plan to be an angel cat after I die, if I am not already. My pet mom has a cat necklace she wears. I know it reminds her of me and I am honored.

Love is the bond that flows forever; let us all remember that. Even though I will be off of this earthly plane - remember, dear pet mom, I shall still be here in spirit, simply living in another dimension.

Remember me when you notice a stray cat or are visited by a flock of birds or discover a butterfly in your garden. Sometimes I may even bounce around on your bed or visit you in your dreams. Take a moment to tune in, listen and feel. You might be surprised. Nothing is

Karla and Pierre

ever really lost, especially love. Thank you, readers, for listening to my stories. I love everyone. Meow meow meooooooooooow.

Pierre

Saying Goodbye

Karla's Celestial Thoughts

I told Pierre over the weekend that I realized he was not feeling well, he must move on and I had to let him go. I told him I had finished the book and was so happy it was done. I also told him there would never be another pet in my life whom I could love and care about so deeply. I knew he had been hanging on, waiting for me to get this project done and I felt a bit selfish because he truly was not well.

Last summer when we nearly lost him, I became aware that Pierre was on borrowed time. A month ago he had a sort of last hurrah. He became especially demanding of my time, butting me with his head if I did not stop whatever I was doing and pay attention to him. He wanted lots of treats, tapping his paw on my leg to be sure he got them. He was Poopsie at his best, alive and full of personality.

Then about two weeks ago, his body started breaking down and he lost weight quickly. His last three days here he was unable to eat. I could no longer deny that the end was near. He was very tired and withdrawn. I slept on my bed with him tucked safely in his little cat bed beside me.

On February 5, 2003, I was emailing my daughter Hazel in Paris, and Pierre was sleeping in his bed. Hazel was the child who was closest to Pierre. After a freak accident while home visiting us, she had been able to spend several extra months with him as she recuperated from a broken wrist and prepared for her trip to France. I think the timing was fortuitous, even though the healing process was difficult for Hazel and fraught with challenges.

As I finished the message to my daughter, Pierre jumped off of the bed, onto a stool, then onto the floor and came directly to my side, tapping me on the leg. I picked him up and in an instant he had a seizure. I held him, although it was difficult, as he shook uncontrollably for a few long minutes. It was awful. His eyes were wild with fear and his heart was racing. I knew he was very frightened.

When the seizure ended he let out two awful moans, the worst I have ever heard from an animal. I held him and cried quietly, not wanting to upset him more. While holding him tightly in my arms, I phoned my veterinarian, asking her to please come over as quickly as possible. She assured me she would be at my door as soon as she finished with her client.

In the meantime Betty, a dear friend who works with Reiki healing, came over. We have a weekly appointment to work together and although we had thought about canceling it this day, we kept our date. Together we performed Reiki healing energy work on Pierre and eased his pain. We talked to him, explaining what was happening to him, encouraging him to let go. I assured him I would be okay, that even though I would miss him, I knew he was hanging on for me and needed to move on.

Animals are so loyal. They sometimes think they should never leave us. Helping our pets experience a merciful death is a gift we can give them to thank them for all they give us. I knew that another Birman named Harrah, a relative of Pierre's that passed on to the other side a few years ago, was going to meet him. I had previously experienced flashes of communication from this cat on the other side.

I was so glad I was not alone that day. My friend Betty, who is also intuitive, was picking up many of the same things I was. It was a beautiful experience. We received information about many of Pierre's past lives, sharing what we were having flashes about, feeling him become calm and still as we worked together to quiet him down.

Even though Pierre had severe cataracts and could not see very well, I told him that the angels were coming to bring him home and he raised up his head and looked upward like he was truly seeing something. It was so amazing, this actually happened! I am so glad I was there for this transition with my angel cat.

When my vet arrived she told me my options after examining Pierre. She explained that his body was jaundiced and was shutting down. The likelihood of continued seizures and pain made it clear to me that it was time. I went into another room with Pierre and explained everything to him, holding him in my lap.

When I knew we were both ready, I carried him into the living room where Betty and the doctor waited. Sitting on the sofa, I cradled Pierre as the vet gave him the shot that helped his body let go. Pierre was very relaxed and passed away quickly. He died in my arms peacefully.

The next day I knew I would get a message from him letting me know he was okay. I had taken the day off from work and was wandering around the house when I heard a woodpecker knocking on the window in my bathroom. The woodpecker in my Angel Star Cards means to focus in, work hard, know things are okay, do your own thing and move on. I have had a number of mystical messages from woodpeckers while working on my books and other creative projects.

I knew this was a message from Pierre! I walked into the bathroom and there was his picture on the wall next to the window where the bird was pecking. I noticed the picture and cried with tears of happiness streaming down my face, knowing it was him coming through with a message. A feeling of peace flowed through my body from head to foot. I knew everything was okay - he was okay. It was a wonderful moment of confirmation that I had done the right thing. Pierre, you are forever with me in my heart.

Each pet we have is different and special in its own way. We can never really replace a pet, each animal is different, but sometimes if we are lucky we may have a reincarnated pet who comes twice. I feel blessed that this happened for me, with Pierre. This book honors him and I will never, ever forget him!

Paw Prints from Pierre

In your heart and soul, I have left my paw print,
Forever bonded by my imprint.
I am a shining new star in the sky,
So stretch out like a cat
And remember me
As you reach up high.

I tried to teach
But did not preach.
By example, I was here.
Love is the ingredient
We all should hold most dear.

Have faith and the courage of a lion,
And always keep on trying.

People and creatures forever bond,
Here and far beyond.
I tried to show you all of my love,
I send sweet blessings from above!

Pierre

Sweet Pierre

Double Gifts - Double Dreams

Eleven days after Pierre died, I had the opportunity to visit a home with my sister where there were two eight year old Himalayan cats, Cosmo and Dharma, which the owners were putting up for adoption. The two small children in the house had no patience and were not compatible with them. It was a difficult situation but I was so moved by these two cats and their plight and also their energies seemed to be so in tune with me when I picked them up and held them that I felt Pierre was helping me with the decision to take them.

Now, a year later, they have come out of their shells and are a delight, and a great comfort to me. Although it took a long time to socialize them, I know Pierre helped. I made the right decision by keeping them.

This year, on February 5th, Pierre appeared to me in a dream. I had not dreamed about him for this entire past year, although I had felt him around many times. I found out the next day that Hazel had dreamed about him the same night! She had not dreamed about him in the past year either, and did not know this was the day he died, a year ago.

We had been very vigilant when Pierre was alive, and aware that we must not let him outside as it would be so difficult for him to cope, and he would have been so frightened. Hazel worried in her dream that he had gone outside and she was very afraid he was in trouble. She awakened with the immediate remembrance that he was dead and was relieved that he was not lost somewhere!

I dreamed the same thing but the dream went further. I thought he had gotten outside too, and I could not find him. I walked outside and suddenly the dream changed and it was summer. There were people all around but I was looking on the ground, trying to see if Pierre was hiding somewhere. It was a warm, sunny day. There was a huge round table in the middle of the yard, along with many square card tables set up for some kind of party. The guests were all standing around outside but not seated at the tables yet. No one seemed to realize I was there.

I felt somehow I would find Pierre hiding under the large round table so I lifted the white table cloth and peeked under it. Sure enough, there was Pierre! I found him! He was lying very peacefully under the table and the grass appeared very green and lush under there, as the whole area seemed to glimmer and shine. There was one post in the middle of the table which held it up. Pierre was on the left side, relaxed, and facing two cats on the right side. I looked more closely and realized the other cats were none other than Cosmo and Dharma! They were facing Pierre and also looking peaceful and serene, like they were all old friends! The feeling was that they were family. They all knew each other in Spirit!

I awakened with a feeling of peace and felt the dream to be a validation that these cats did indeed know each other somehow. I realized once again that Pierre is okay on the other side, and knows Cosmo and Dharma are here with me now. In fact, I think it was all part of a plan and that he sent them to me.

I feel so grateful to Pierre who continues to be a powerful force in my life, and this was his gift to me once again - two Himalayan cats, so I would not be alone. Love continues on eternally. Thank you again, sweet Pierre.

Karla, Pet Mom

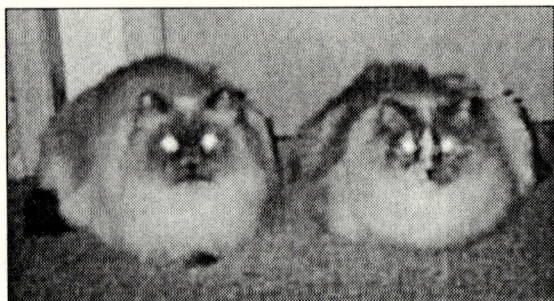

Cosmo and Dharma

Hazel and Cosmo

Hazel and Dharma

Information on Karla Wessel

An intuitive reader, artist, and author, Karla Wessel has created a business designed around her spiritual gifts. She is currently working on the second in this series of books about using intuition, filled with more mystical stories. Also, she is recreating her Angel Star Cards which will be reproduced in 2006.

Feel free to contact Karla about Intuitive Readings for groups, parties, or special events, or for information on her popular classes covering the many ways to become more intuitive—like interpreting dreams, meditation, messages from nature, finding your own spirit guides and Guardian Angel, automatic writing, numerology, astrology, Reiki, and Feng Shui.

Karla also does intuitive life coaching with a limited number of students, one-on-one.

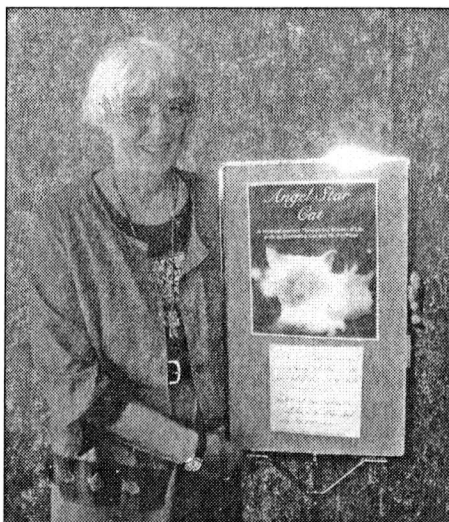

Karla at first Book Signing.

If anyone wishes to write to the author, the address is:
Karla Wessel
P. O. Box 626
Forest Lake, Minnesota 55025
Website: www.angelstarjourneys.com
E mail: angelstarjourneys@yahoo.com

Karla's book is so interesting, insightful and true, as it is about real people. Her family must be beaming with pride about her, and her talents. Also she gave me such a powerful reading, the other day—what a gifted person she is. –Nancie Lauritsen, St. Paul, MN

I have known Karla for many years, and think she is one of the best, intuitively, and as a good friend. I think her book is going to awaken a lot of people to understand the importance of the animal/people connections. –Betty Harmen, Maplewood, MN

I love Karla's book because of its honesty and insights. My intuitive coaching experience with Karla has also been amazing. I have gained a deeper understanding of myself and my metaphysical side. I've also come to have a better understanding of others. Karla's teaching is perceptive and spiritual. I'd recommend it to anyone looking to deepen their self-awareness and/or their "sixth sense"! - Jennifer Longinow, Woodbury, MN

Printed in the United States
44639LVS00003B/1-159

9 781593 302757